MW01181328

EXTREME

an anthology for social and environmental justice

Selection/Edition by Mark Lipman

VAGABOND

Vagabond
Venice, California

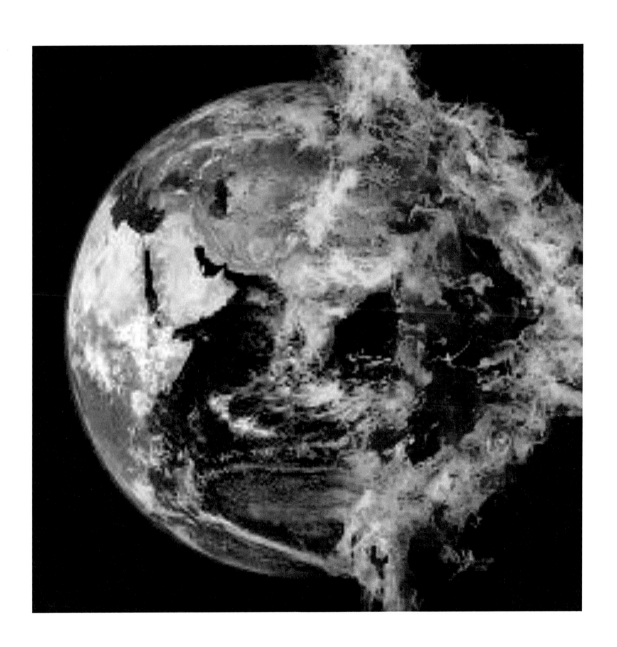

FAIR USE NOTICE

Edition Copyright © 2018 by Mark Lipman, editor
Front cover art based on *Earth on Fire*, unknown artist;
Revolution, by Mear One and *Global Warming*, by Wieslaw Smetek
Back cover art based on the *The War Against Nature*, by Mark Bryan.
All rights reserved.

editor@vagabondbooks.net

Published by VAGABOND
Mark Lipman, editor

VAGABOND Collection

Intellectual Property
reverts back to the individual poet / artist upon publication.
EXTREME (an anthology for social and environmental justice)
1st ed. / p.cm.

ISBN 13: 978-1-936293-31-5

Made in the USA.

"Power to the people, stick it to the man."
~ Captain Fantastic

TABLE OF CONTENTS

10 ~ Forward: As the Pendulum Swings, by Mark Lipman

FORWARD

AS THE PENDULUM SWINGS

"There's nothing to fear, but fear itself."
~ Franklin Delano Roosevelt

Now, as the pendulum swings from side to side, from right to left and back again, we are faced with the stark realization that nothing within the spectrum of capitalist left to capitalist right – of what we are allowed to discuss by way of defining the possible – has anything to offer but more failure. Both sides stand for more wars and corporate greed, as the body bags and broken lives stack up on the street corners all across America, while community after community is ravaged by fire and water, with one unnatural disaster after another, whether it be plastic oceans powered by Fukushima, tainted water, lava flows or broken oil roads leading to the next extinct species, or an Arctic on fire, orchestrated to the sounds of yet another round of gunfire in our classrooms, as our children bleed their lives and futures away to the indifference of bigotry and ignorance.

With the center's collapse, the lunatics have truly taken over the asylum and all we are left with is what now lies on the extreme. From the ideological extreme to the extreme weather cycles of global warming, the dystopia we once feared is now upon us. Panic and lethargy however are not options. In times of such global extremism, with the reemergence of fascist and totalitarian governments, now more than ever it is incumbent on all of us, as a people, to stand up, organize and prepare.

No one of us is able to do this alone. There is no superhero who is going to come out of the sky and save the day, nor will some political idol suddenly take up power and fix all our problems with the stroke of a pen. The solutions we need, as a people and society, are only going to come about by countless ordinary people standing up and doing what they can when the moment and opportunity arises to fight injustice and redefine what is possible. That is what we mean when we use the words "Solidarity" and "Together".

Remember, as far as that pendulum swings over to one side, so too will it come just as far back to the other. When the failure of extreme capitalism, the period in which we now find ourselves, is complete, we'll be left with no other option than the ideas and solutions that We the People bring to the table. It's therefore no surprise that the terms "Socialism" and "Democratic Socialism" have likewise become so prevalent today, for that's the future that awaits us not so very far away. When that opportunity presents itself we have to be ready as a people to right those scales of justice, for we may never get another chance.

Power, it is said, never concedes a thing without a fight, we all know this to be true. The struggle seems to always be with us. This is no different. We fight, not because we want to, but because we must – our combined future and very lives depend on it. We fight as an affirmation that we believe in a better future that we have the power to bring into being.

This book, EXTREME (an anthology for social and environmental justice), comes neither at the beginning nor at the end of that struggle, but as a continuation at a critical juncture in time, bringing forth the poetic voices of today in a scope that is both American and international in the same breath, that speaks to who we are at the root of our humanity.

As poets (by which we mean all artists) our duty here is two-fold, to both speak the truth to power, of the reality of the world in which we live, and also to set loose our own imaginations, to dare to let ourselves dream of a better world and way of life that cares equally for the planet on which we live and for those who live on it, for this is how we spark the light within others to make those dreams become a reality.

So yes, we do say that another world, one that is sustainable for future generations, where human rights and our ecology is restored, is not only possible, but inevitable, for it is we, those of us who are writing and reading and living these pages herein, who are going to make it happen, through the power of our words and actions.

Mark Lipman, editor
05 August 2018

ECCE CARMEN

This poem's been
written many, many times
by you, or you or some
other famous poet.

And this poem is
inspired by that other
poem written
by you, or

you or that famous
poet whose name
escapes me at
this moment.

This poem began
when time began
and will last until time
ends. This poem welcomes

with a hearty
hug. It tells
the truth or
blurs it

blind. This poem paints
the skies green.
Turns rivers
into lemonade.

This poem's heavy duty and
kink resistant.
This poem is a dream
like all poems are

dreams so the title of
this poem cannot be
titled *Dream* or
Dreams or *Nightmares*

because those are just
bad dreams. Scorpions
live inside this poem. As do spiders
as do frogs, as do things that go bump in the night.

This poem is evil. This poem is
Harry Powell. This poem is
Norman Bates, Darth Vader,
Hannibal Lecter, Tom Riddle.

This poem is a black man.
This poem gets shot and dies.
This poem is transgender.
This poem can't piss in their toilet.

This poem is Muslim, is Syrian
a refugee, a little boy fleeing
war, drowned in the surf
on a beach in Turkey.

This poem likes men.
This poem is gay.
This poem is SO gay
because I hate poetry

and poems SO MUCH
they suck and they're gay
but this poem
will rip your clothes off

Lee Eric Freeman

or beat you senseless
'til you're
blue, bruised
damaged and *rearranged*.

This poem is Hitler.
This poem is Pol Pot.
This poem is Idi Amin. This
poem is Donald ...

... or it could be
if you or I
wanted it
maybe.

This poem is good.
So good, in fact there's
too much good inside
this poem to call this poem evil.

This poem is Monet.
This poem is Satie.
This poem is Rimbaud.
Ecce Homo! – behold the man!
This poem screams.

You'll love this poem.
You'll hate this poem.
This is the rule
for ALL poems.

This poem makes you reach.
This poem makes you retch.
Makes you feel, makes you think.

But this poem's a fraud

a scam, a lark
a fluke, a fake, a cliché.
It's not a poem.
This poem is as good

as dead until such
time when you or
I read this poem
hear this poem

it'll open its eyes
spread its wings.
This poem's a butterfly.
This poem's

an eagle
a poetry eagle.
This poem will soar.
This poem will

drum the drum
gong the gong
horn the horn.
This poem will roar

raise the roof
take the action
stand up, fight back;
Ecce Carmen! – behold the poem!
This poem is
            to be ...
            ... continued.

HOLLOW

6, 10, 12, 14, 26, 32, 49, 58
The death count ticks upward
like a spastic taxi meter.

Quickly the casualties rise
26, 32, 49, 58 the latest
worst mass shooting in America

as yet, another city or town
joins the club of
I never thought it could happen here.

Here.   Here.   Here.   Here.
Here.   Here.   Here.   Here.
Here.   Here.   Here.   Here.
There.   There.   There.   There.

Dear US government
how many more
mass killings

must happen Here and There
before you get off
your fat lazy ass?

Your congressional moments
of silence
your presidential
visits of healing
your half-staff
flags
ring hollow.

Your inactions are
unspeakable evil.

Your heads are hollow
your hearts are hollow.

San Ysidro.
Columbine.
Killeen.
Newtown.
Charleston.
Chattanooga.
Roseburg.
Orlando.
Las Vegas.

The list goes on, the club grows larger
the stakes set higher and higher.
Your wallets grow fatter

your stomachs grow
fatter from bribing
lobbyists whose endless

supplies of cash and steaks
is equal to their endless
supplies of guns and bullets.

Death never takes a holiday.
Will you and your family holiday
on your own private island far
far away? How about an
all-inclusive trip to Mandalay Bay?
The 32nd floor is nice, so they say.

Guns don't kill
people, people kill people.

Lee Eric Freeman

15

The only thing that stops
a bad guy with a gun,
is a good guy with a gun.
..., the right of the people
to keep and bear arms...

And who protects
the rights of the dead
who bear no arms?

Not you, not you, not you
my US government
of the People.

Your prayers do nothing
your vigils do nothing
your flag waves do nothing.

your conduct does nothing
your nothing speaks volumes.

You loosen your belt
you do nothing.

You are deaf.
You are dumb.
You are blind.

You are hollow.

Lee Eric Freedman is the 3rd Poet Laureate of Swampscott,
Massachusetts (2016-2018). Since 2011 he's been affectionately entitled
as the *Renegade Poet Laureate of Swampscott.* He is truly honored and
humbled to be both. When Lee isn't busy being any type of Laureate he
leads the *Tin Box Poets of Swampscott Workshop Group* and regularly
performs at open-mics all over the place. Lee is coauthor of *Mad Men of
Lynn, Writings from the Walnut Street Coffee Cafe* (Ring of Bone Press) and
is a three time winner of the Naomi Cherkofsky Memorial Poetry Contest.
He resides in Swampscott, MA.

BREAD AND BANDAGES

to Kurdish women

Let's go beyond
disseminating info/facebook photos

send school buses\help new businesses
send baking equipment/run English classes

no bread left in Afrin country
no Left left in fascist country

raise voices/raise funds
time to be aware
women fighters die from blood loss
waiting for care

it's not a possibility
it's a necessity

let's send hemostatic dressings
let's go make bread and bandages
to stop bleeding from
fascism
patriarchy
capitalism

Let's go beyond all
Let's go to Rojava and Shengal!

Serena Piccoli

LIBERTÉ/EGALITÉ/FRATERNITÉ/ CRIME DE SOLIDARITÉ

(Scritta il 25 marzo 2018, dopo la morte di Destinity, il rimpatrio di un'altra famiglia nigeriana e la guida alpina umanitaria Benoit che rischia 5 anni di carcere per il reato di solidarietà.)

Liberté

Mi chiamo Destinity, il mio bimbo è in me da 7 mesi

anche il tumore e ho perso lavoro in Italia

ho conosciuto la parola neve

qui arranco sui monti

verso la Francia:

vado da mia sorella.

///

Égalité

"I bambini sono tutti uguali"

da 8 mesi ho il terzo in me

marciamo

mio marito con Omar in braccio

sui monti:

non voglio che i miei piccoli

raccolgano cobalto in miniera

per i telefoni dei bianchi.

///

skilift/skipass/

trekking/rafting/

NO TRESPASSING/

Serena Piccoli

18

LIBERTÉ/EGALITÉ/FRATERNITÉ/ CRIME DE SOLIDARITÉ

(Written on March 25th 2018, after the death of Destinity – a Nigerian woman, the repatriation of another Nigerian family from France and after the case of the Alpine humanitarian French guide – Benoit – who risks up to 5 years of imprisonment for the so-called Crime of Solidarity – enforced in France – which punishes those who help for the entry, movement and residence of immigrants.)

Liberté

I'm Destinity, my baby's been in me for 7 months
so has cancer. I've lost my job in Italy
now I know the word snow
I limp on mountains
to France:
to my sister's.
///

Égalité

"Children are all the same"
Have had the third in me for 8 months
marching
Omar in my husband's arms
on Alps:
I don't want my kids
mining cobalt
for whites' smartphones.
///
skilift/skipass/
trekking/rafting/
NO TRESPASSING/

Serena Piccoli

19

///

Nella sabbia mobile bianca

zoppico

respiro a fatica

dio aiutami

la pancia pesa

sfinita

il gelo schiaccia

dio aiutami

mi prende in braccio

siamo tutti sull'auto in corsa

bianca sul bianco ovunque

dentro me

mi dà nausea

dio aiutami

l'Uomo della Neve, come lo chiama mio marito

ferma l'auto

in mezzo al bianco niente

grida scende

contorta tra il pianto dei bimbi

grida "*hopital*" e altri gli urlano.

"*No. Non abbiamo documenti*"

dio aiutami

/ / /

In the White quicksand
limping
hardly breathing
godhelpme
heavy belly
exhausted
chill running in me
godhelpme
he carries me
we're all in the fast car
white on the White everywhere
in me
makes me sick
godhelpme
SnowMan, as my husband calls him
stops the car
in the middle of the White nowhere
shouting/getting off
writhed on White and kids'cries
he shouts "*hopital*" and others shout.

"*No. We have no papers*"
godhelpme

21

Benoit/Uomo della Neve è bloccato dalla polizia
e da 5 possibili anni di prigionia
ho in braccio il mio terzo figlio
saremo spediti subito indietro
voglio solo che il mio piccolo Benoit
non finisca in miniera.
/ / /
La neve è luce nel buio della nostra marcia
questo mondo bianco mi dà nausea
ci bloccano in Francia
ci abbandonano in Italia
3 di notte chiusa la stazione dei treni
io mio marito il mio bimbo dentro
senza aiuto fuori
arriverà il giorno
arriverà qualcuno.

Ormai la luce sui vetri nasce
e io muoio di voi.

Benoit/SnowMan is halted by police
and by 5 possible years in prison
my third son is in my arms
we'll be quickly sent back home
I only want my baby Benoit
not end up mining.
/ / /
The snow is the light in the darkness of our march
this White world makes me sick
they stop us in France
abandon in Italy
3 a.m. the railway station's closed
I my husband my baby in me
no help outside
the day will come
and someone will.

The light on glasses nearly appears
while I'm disappearing for you.

Serena Piccoli is an Italian award winning poet, playwright and translator (English, French, Italian) and cultural liaison, organizing and marketing international art events and performance touts through Italy (where she lives). She is the co-founder and director (along with poet Giorgia Monti) of the well acclaimed Poetry and Sister Arts International Festival (Forlì-Cesena, Italy). With her book of political poems against Trump and Berlusconi (former Italian prime minister) "*silviotrump*", Serena Piccoli is the only Italian poet in the Locofo Chaps, a politically-oriented poetry series edited by poet William Allegrezza (Moria poetry, Chicago, USA).

23

Mother Earth's Teardrops

Mother Earth

Hear me now

I am not the one beating you down

Okay maybe a little

But not nearly like the others

The others

Whose trash I pick up

The others whose glass, cans, and cardboard

I recycle

I plan my errands so that I make one trip

Versus

Multiple unnecessary trips throughout the week

I save your tear drops in my water tank

I can show you

Come look

Your tears feed my plants

My plants feed me

Reduce

Reuse

Recycle

They say

That's the name of the game

Lee Thunders

2018,
The Current State

We're all fucked
Manufacture electric car
Mother Earth carbon drugged
The same, if not more

Plug in
Charge car
From wind and solar
You're in luck

Mine minerals
Batteries need, tick
Human rights violation, tick
Ecological devastation

Battery won't charge
Store underground
Join the nuke juice
Seepage to sea and land

Intermingle fertilizer and pesticide
Underground aquifer
Contamination
But we have to eat!

And what about the bees?
Pollination abolition
Will there be food
In years to come?

Continuing the talk on eating
I heard that methane
From cow farming
Is burps versus farts

What about drinking?
Plastic bottles
One million sold every minute
We're all fucked

Lee Thunders is a Los Angeles musician, writer, and avid rainwater harvester.

Lee Thunders

25

State of the Union

*Man has no right to kill his brother. It is no excuse
that he does so in uniform; he only adds the infamy
of servitude to the crime of murder.*
~ Percy Shelly (19th Century)

Innocent victims whose weapons are seduced
by the grease of ignorant contraband have become
smugglers in the night. Rages of avarice pay wages
for the art of war. Proud assassins assemble around
graves profaned by military loons and cougars. Look
at that invading sparrow! Its toes tighten on

tethered twigs, as National Endowment spies tell lies
that make us die for prizes: blood money, war money
all honored in the enemy camp. Literary bureaucrats
embalming our integrity. We are frozen in library
morgues of corporate bribery. They are railroading
writers in genocide of a weapons contest. Soon, we

will not have any more prayers, adventures, values,
morals, ideals or dreams to determine what a
living Hell it really is and Heaven is crowded with
quotidian clouds of discontent. When will the 1,000
years cumulous feast begin? Sinister schemes to turn
nuclear war into a video game to dynamite and dam

the rapture. Whether it was to defoliate Southeast
Asian villages or Middle-Eastern desert sands

there are just too many idiot fingers squeezing
with the same predatory designs for aggression as
that sparrow's bivouac with insensitive toes on
triggers.

Michael C Ford

27

FOR WHOMEVER PLANS TO DISHONOR YET ANOTHER AMERICAN PRESIDENCY

Vote for no one who supports ignorant genealogy
Nor one who would blast open space of our astrology
Nor would pollute with acid rains our climatology
Nor encourage the war mongers of our pathology
Nor strip-mine the fertile gifts of our geology
Nor bury salutary necessities of our petrology
Nor poison the saviors of our ecology
Nor drown civilian values of our hydrology
Nor swim against the tides of our oceanography
Nor would bulldoze the Earth of our cartography
Nor corrupt the eco-system trees of our topography

Or will our new Commander-In-Chief of the free world,
In opposition to the old dogs of democracy, truly be
An anti-Demo-Republican Green advocate whose
Vision of Equality is, as no other in our national
History, be listening to us puppies in militant barking
Protest against electing, yet, another harbinger of
Hypocrisy, endlessly, participating in a conspiracy to
Commit Constitutional rape?

Photo by: Alexis Rhone-Fancher

Michael C Ford has been publishing steadily, since 1970, and credited with over 28 volumes of print documents. He's been featured on approx. 70 spoken word tracks that include California Artists Radio Theatre productions plus 4 solo documents, since 1985. His debut vinyl received a Grammy nomination [1987] and his Selected Poems earned a Pulitzer nomination on the 1st ballot [1998]. Hen House Studios has been promoting and marketing his CD project Look Each Other in the Ears [2014]. That document, in both vinyl and CD formats features a stellar band of musicians, not the least of which were surviving members of a 1960s theatre rock quartet that most of you will remember as The Doors.

Michael C Ford

AMERICAN DREAMS AND
NIGHTMARES

Was it a mechanised or human alarm,
some media lines
you took as a warning
that brought you out on your gated balcony
with your binoculars, telescope?

Was it a shadow,
just an image?
A real or imagined
prowler?

Did you construct him black
inside your skull;
like the"thug" talked to a one day life
by a woman who murdered her children?
But I am your other nightmare.

I awake one morning
next to a chess board
as a horseman
with horse power,
speed, and vertical leap.

A voice tells me I have 24 hours
before returning to my natural state.

I am your other nightmare.
Jumping the fence
two gallups forward
one left
into your perimeter.

You will wonder sometime
"Was this at sunset or dawn?"
Was it a fantasy you dusk dreamed
while waiting for dinner?
Were your eyes closed, moving rapidly?
Or was it real?

I dash past your window,
a blur
and I'm gone.
I am your other nightmare.

I am
the Caucasian Jockey
who will not sit on your lawn
sipping a cocktail
with your shots of feel superior
that your servant poured and blended
with the booz and crushed ice.

Jerry Pendergast

With ears sucking in
your nutra sweetened cliches,
drama from a replayed alarm
that taxes my Psyche.

I will fling question marks
in front of you
when you rail against undesireables

when you voice command me
with evidence manufactured
from repetition,
to attack an enemy I have not met.

I observe
but do not absorb
your pathetic white man wink,

the three finger W,
the pinky and thumb P,
from the hand of your hired mouthpiece/thug.

I see no legitimate power
only a toilet symbol
from a bad childhood joke.

Chicago Street Names Historical Names and the Black and Green Connection

Monroe:
5th President of the United States.
Hosted Dinner, Lunch and sometimes breakfast seminars
for rich white guys.

Wrote up a doctrine,
still used as an excuse to call Latin America
and the Caribbean Islands
"OUR BACK YARD".
Employed African Americans.

A street in Chicago
running east and West
2300 block the scene of an assassination in 1969
of one man age 22, another 21.

Clarke
A street in Chicago that was once a shoreline.
Runs North and South.
Angles slightly West.
Later a Potawatomie trail.
Primarily a commercial street.

Mark Clark:
Assassinated with Fred Hampton.
They were officers
in the Black Panther Party Illinois.
Helped some gangs negotiate truces
Ran a Breakfast program for Hungry kids.

Jerry Pendergast

31

Assessed as a threat
to "OUR NATION"
from an FBI office.

Tom Clarke:
Planned the Easter Rising
with Padraig Pearce
in Dublin in 1916.
Captured and killed
by the British Army.

Hugh O'Neal:
Irish Chieftain.
Led uprisings
against British rule.

William O'Neal:
FBI informant.
Laced Fred Hampton's dinner drink
with barbiturates
on the night of the assassination.

Hampton Court
Street running North and south,
close to Lincoln Park.
Has new Luxury Apartments
on its 2700 block.

Edward Hanrahan:
Illinois state's Attorney
indicted for raid
that killed Hampton and Clark
December 1969.
No street is named after him.

Jerry Pendergast is a lifelong Cook County resident, who grew up across the street from Ronald McDonald House on Deming place when it was the St. Clement Convent. The Mid North Side of Chicago was more working class then. He is a graduated from Northeastern Illinois and lives with his wife Kathleen in the North Park area of Chicago. They have two sons. One lives in Sheffield England. Our younger lives in the Albany Park area. He's been writing for over 40 years and currently hosts an Open Mic series at Gallery Cabaret in the Wicker Park area, every 2nd and 4th Tuesday.

THERE'S A BRAINSTORM IN WASHINGTON

There's a brainstorm in Washington, Vosnesensky reports,
and all the a-holes are in imminent danger

All the war mongers, armament, sugar, rifle
association and what not lobbyists

Even the biggest a-hole of them all
appears to be in imminent danger

God bless America and may it rid itself
of its very own worst to become great

ES BRAUT SICH EIN WAHRHEITSSTURM IN WASHINGTON ZUSAMMEN

Es braut sich ein Wahrheitssturm in Washington zusammen, berichtet Wosnessenski,
und alle A-Löcher sind in unmittelbarer Gefahr

Alle die Kriegstreiber, die Lobbyisten für die Rüstungsindustrie,
für den unbegrenzten Besitz von Waffen, die Zuckerindustrie und so weiter

Sogar das größte A-Loch überhaupt
schwebt in unmittelbarer Gefahr

Gott segne Amerika, und möge es sich von den Schlimmsten
der Schlimmen befreien, um tatsächlich groß zu werden

Johannes Beilharz writes in German and English, paints, takes
pictures, translates, absorbs the news, cooks and lives in Rome.

Johannes Beilharz

33

GUERRA

1.
No conozco la guerra,
sólo la he visto en filmes
aunque mi vida no sea más
que uno de sus efectos.

Me atrevo, sin embargo, a juzgarla:
culpar a quien con hábiles excusas
exige nuestros vítores y aplausos
por los supuestos triunfos de una Idea,
una Fe, una Nación
que nunca he visto consumarse.

Dichoso por no haberla sufrido en carne propia,
me ha bastado mirar en alta definición
el rostro de un actor o un veterano
             – de fondo los sollozos
de una viuda y sus huérfanos –
para aprender
que los credos de hoy serán mañana
pretexto para nuevas asechanzas, baldía
sinrazón en unos tanto como en otros.

No conozco la guerra, pero creo
saber sin esperanza
por qué y por quiénes siempre
nos sobrevive.

2.
Puede que haya días
en que no escuchemos
los partes de guerra,
pero ella continúa
más allá de nosotros.

Jesús J. Barquet

34

WAR

1.
I do not know war,
I have only seen it in films
although my life is no more
than one of its effects.

But I dare to judge it,
blame whomever with skillful pretexts
requires our cheers and applauses
for the alleged triumphs of an Idea,
a Faith, a Nation
that I have never seen achieved.

Lucky for not suffering it physically,
it was enough for me to watch in high definition
any actor's or veteran's face
– in the background a widow
and her orphans wailing –
to learn
that today's doctrines will be tomorrow's
pretenses for new entrapments, pointless
excuses for some as much as for others.

I do not know war, but believe I know
without hope
why and by whom it always survives us.

2.
There may be days
when we do not listen to
the news on war,
but it endures
beyond us.

Translation by Beth Pollack and the author

Jesús J. Barquet was born in Havana in 1953 and went into exile in
the United States in 1980 as part of the Mariel exodus. His books of
poetry include *Aguja de diversos* (2018), *Venturous Journeys / Los viajes
venturosos* (2015), *Cuerpos del delirio (Sumario poético 1971-2008)*
(2010), *Sin fecha de extinción* (2004), *Naufragios* (Honorary Mention in
Gastón Baquero Prize, 1998), *Un no rompido sueño* (Second Prize of
Chicano / Latino Poetry, 1994), *Sagradas herejías* (1985) and *Sin decir
el mar* (1981). Co-editor of the anthologies *Poesía cubana del siglo XX*
(2002) and *Todo parecía: poesía cubana contemporánea de temas gays
y lésbicos* (2015). Author of the critical compilation *Ediciones El Puente en La Habana de los años
60* (2011) and *Consagración de La Habana* (Letras de Oro Prize in Essay, 1992). He's currently
Professor Emeritus of New Mexico State University and director of La Mirada Editions.

Jesús J. Barquet

35

THE "F" WORD

The notices had come three weeks
earlier, spilling their venom
across the kitchen table and
the ugly sign posted on the lawn.
But Marta could not get herself to respond –
as if by putting off knowing
what she knew, putting off doing
what she knew she had to do,
her life would continue as normal.

Tonight, she tucks in the kids, avoiding
the thought that this is their last night
in this house, this bed, maybe
even with this parent, as she briefly
contemplates blowing out her brains.
José goes from room to room,
caressing the cabinets he constructed,
the wallpaper he hung in the hall,
stooping to touch the tiles he installed
on the kitchen floor and the patio.
He feels as if he were sleepwalking,
that he will awaken with the sun
warming him through the open window,
the children running in, as always,
jumping on the bed, laughing.

At dawn, when they least expect it,
though they've been dreading it for
the past 24 hours, four men, burly, resolute,
break down the front door, yelling
Now! Everybody up! Move!

Before they can take a deep breath
the men push them out of the house, their
stained mattresses, sofa, the crib,
shoes, pots and pans, dishes, underwear,
baby photos – the intimacy of their lives –
dumped on the lawn of the world. The men
shackle the door, post a FORECLOSURE
sign in the grass, and drive away.

The baby cries. José hides his head in
his hands, his Army medals glinting
in the pink light. Ana, the oldest,
leans against him, while her brother
sits on the grass, playing with his skates.
Marta looks around, stunned.
Maybe they should have sought help –
but from whom? And where to go?
Neighbors watch them through
half-closed blinds, afraid. And all
around them, the greedy hordes in wait.

Gloria Vando

WHEN WE TALK ABOUT WAR

I see a child, maimed, hungry,
weeping over his mother's body.
He sees a football field, line backers
tackling opponents. I see loss.
He sees advantage, territory.
I hear the gold harp's silence.
He hears the drone of oil rigs
across the landscape his men
have taken. I see the press
embedded with the government.
He watches Fox and cheers
our progress. Wisely,
we never talk about God.

Gloria Vando's books and poems have won numerous awards, including the Poetry Society of America's Di Castagnola Award, the Latino Literary Hall of Fame's Poetry Book Award, *River Styx* International Poetry Award, and others. She has served as literature panelist for the NEA and various State Arts Councils, and as judge for the National Poetry Series and other contests. She is founding publisher/editor of Helicon Nine Editions, for which she received the Governor's Arts Award (KS), contributing editor to the *North American Review,* co-founder of The Writers Place, a literary center in Kansas City, and serves on the boards of the Venice Arts Council and Beyond Baroque.

Gloria Vando

DISNEYLAND AND THE COPS

for Susan Lamont

Napolean on The Delaware
A comic strip by Delacroix

Bullets collide in the air
Mercury, Venus, Mars, Jupiter

and Saturn are about to align
Or was that The Civil War?

Or Desert *Sturm und Drang*?
The market primed for a rally

Long live Superman!
Donald Duck on the shores of Tripoli

Infinite Justice or Divine Intervention?
Who invented Everyman?

     "Get on the ground!
Hands behind your back

     Stop resisting!
I didn't *know* you were black..."

Talk about every life matters
The bending of the bow

and when the bow breaks
She was so beautiful in her rhythm

and robes. Her flame and pose
Liberty, *come on-a my house.*

Michael Rothenberg

39

THE TRUMPETERS

Cowards in white sheets, the skinhead cops
and racists, the religious working men
and women who think a woman's place is
in the kitchen and children are to be seen
and not heard, and believe people of color
are here in America as a privilege not a right,
who blame Obama for 9/11, but he wasn't
even president then, the ones who say racism
didn't exist in America until Obama,
the blowhards, The Trumpeters, the ones
who will murder to be in the driver's seat
of a big white capitalist car, who will never
be in the driver's seat, will always be
second-rate white people, in the rich
man's eye, they might as well be black
for their marginalized existence in the grand
scheme of the upper class American
power elite, but still they buy into the lie,
with their heads up the ass of the real oppressors,
the powerful whites who will never share
a piece of the pie with their middle-class
and working class, poor white cousins, who
only see these ordinary folk, these regular
people as grist for the mill, unruly ignorants
who they can use to help them build their
oligarchic empires, the front line of their
marching band, The Trumpeters, blowing
the horn of oppression, blowing the horn
of the white man's dream to rule the world,
the white man's dream to carry guns
in the street, free to murder kids in Sandy Hook,
free to beat their wives, and practice rape
as a contact sport while they graduate
from Stanford University with a big white
degree, free to treat a woman as property,

Michael Rothenberg

like a piece of shit, these Trumpeters, they blow,
and blow hard, The Trumpeters, the 40 percent,
maybe 50 percent of America, who will sell
their souls for the promise of ever-elusive
power, the good old Christians who spit
in Christ's face and rape him on the cross,
the ones that covet cruelty, The Trumpeters,
the patriotic Trumpeters, the ones who think
the USA is a page in an owner's manual,
clear as day, that they can own democracy,
rig and twist justice and truth to their
self-interested lies and aspirations, that justice
can be bought and sold, as long as white
people rule the world, The Trumpeters,
the ones who think the USA is a big fucking
TV set, as they slurp down their supersized
cans of pharmaceutical sugar and poison,
The Trumpeters, who mimic some hallmark
illusion of The Great White American Way,
and lick the boots of a reality show star,
The Trumpeters, may they suffer the pain
they wish on the poor, the weak, the abandoned,
and rot in the hell of their own vanity,
greed, envy, pride, lust, and sloth and ten
more sins that are their legacy, the sins of
The Trumpeters! Oh, Trumpeters, come on,
blow, blow, blow, your trumpets, here
comes your monster daddy, he comes to give
you another script to read because you can't
think for yourselves, and he will fuck you
in the ass, and he will never kiss you, never
ever be like you, or with you, he will only
bleed you, and bleed you, fodder for his wars,
fodder for his ecocidal factories, fodder
for his machineries of deception, yes, you
will be his robot army, because you are,

accept it, only Trumpeters, only soulless slaves,
at your very core, behind your brassiness
you are only a procession of cowards, and you
will follow and pronounce your yahoo
independence as you walk to your hate-filled
grave, you will follow the goosestep of the
high boot and genocide, get in line proud
Trumpeters, the future is yours, there's a banquet
waiting for you beyond the gates of Valhalla,
come on, you are the lucky ones, the entitled ones,
not only the desired guest for the feast, you are
the feast itself, so bow down and open your collar,
your red-haired father is coming to devour you.

Michael Rothenberg is the editor of BigBridge.org and co-founder of
100 Thousand Poets for Change (www.100tpc.org). His most recent
books of poetry include *Drawing The Shade* (Dos Madres Press, 2016),
Wake Up and Dream (MadHat Press, 2017), and a bi-lingual edition
of *Tally Ho and The Cowboy Dream / The Real and False Journals*
(Varasek Ediciones, Madrid Spain, 2018). He lives in Tallahassee,
Florida.

OPPONENTS CHARLOTTESVILLE 2017

THEY DESPISE US
TO THE CORE.

Our statues
They hate,
Our flags
They hate,
Our heritage
They hate,
Our culture
They hate.
They'd rather have
Our First World
Turn into
The Third World
Of immigrants,
Have faces in
The media
Be darker ones,
Have faces at the top
Be darker ones.
We want to
Turn the clock
Back to simpler times
Before the mud people
Threaten our
Ethnic future.

WHITE LIVES MATTER.

THEY DESPISE US
TO THE CORE.

Our safety
They threaten,
Our lives
They threaten,
Our struggle
They threaten,
Our races
They threaten.
This is the 21st Century.
We can't believe
We're still
Protesting
This.
Fear, guns & slurs
From the ones preferring
A mirror image of the past.
More division,
More terror,
More being called
"Boy" the older we get.
If you love yourself,
Your people & diversity,
Don't let them
Turn time back.

BLACK LIVES MATTER.

Hatred marches not from
Both sides, only one.

Dee Allen

43

TAINT

The most
Important thing
To the lives
Of the citizens
Of Flint, Michigan,
More important than
The city itself

Pours out of
The chrome faucet
With a very
Strange, pale
Brownish tint

Liquid rust
Flowing lead
At the turn
Of a knob.

Unsafe to drink,
Unsafe to cook with,
Unsafe to bathe in,
Unsafe to live around –

While General Motors©
Has full access
To the cleaner stuff
From Lake Huron,

The most abundant
Source of taint
In the Midwest,
Fluidic, corrosive, septic,

Is available to
All the rest.

Lead in the river,
Lead in a child's blood.

Relief comes from

Outside the stricken Black
Rust Belt city.
Salvation comes contained
In donated plastic
Jugs and bottles,
The corporate scam,
The necessary evil,
Better than nothing

Gives the populace
A running chance.

A thirst-quenching,
Body-cleansing,
Blood-purifying,
Life-restoring
Running chance

Dee Allen

At surviving
A switch in
The water supply,
A government plan,
A lapse in judgement
Costing everyone
Their H2O –

The Dineh Indian
Reservation near mines and
The San Francisco Peaks
Could use the same
Kind of relief, since

Copper, iron, tanzanite, uranium,
Disposed
Pharmaceuticals,
Reused,
Melted
Toilet waste

Found their way
Blended well into
Their own waterways.
A little too
Disturbingly
Reminiscent to

Liquid rust
Flowing lead

River taint

At the turn
Of a knob.

Dee Allen is an African-Italian performance poet based in Oakland, California. Active on the creative writing & Spoken Word tips since the early 1990s. Author of 3 books [*Boneyard, Unwritten Law* and *Stormwater*, all from POOR Press] and 15.5 anthology appearances [including *Poets 11: 2014, Feather Floating On The Water, Rise, Your Golden Sun Still Shines, The City Is Already Speaking* and the newest from MoonShine Star Company, *What Is Love?*] under his figurative belt so far. Dee is in the process of producing his upcoming 4th volume of poetry entitled *Skeletal Black.*

Sea of Oil, Ship of Fools

The EXXON VALDEZ steamed through the rocks and shoals
of Prince William Sound,
through waters darker than the oil
that filled the hold of the ship
and expanded the slick bank accounts of the company chiefs.

It was just past midnight,
and the overworked crew dreamed
of a well-earned drink at their port of call
in Long Beach, California.

Meanwhile, the wildlife that made
this remote Alaskan shore their keep
dreamed of morsels of herring and feasts of silver salmon,
and readied themselves for animal sleep.

At 12:04 a.m., the jagged spikes of Bligh's Reef
sliced open the heart of the *EXXON VALDEZ,*
and 11 million gallons of jet-black crude
poured into the night sea,
a sticky blanket not yet seen
that washed ashore with the onrushing tide.

The *EXXON VALDEZ* was a floating time bomb,
steered by a ship of fools,
detonated by an unsafe collision
of corporate rules.

Exxon Shipping Company failed to supervise
the Master and Commander,
fast asleep in his captain's bunk
after warming his bloodstream on the drunk.

The downsized crew were like worker bees,
carrying the black gold that was Exxon's honey

46 **Henry Howard**

in shifts up to fourteen hours long,
rushing to leave Valdez with a boatload of money.

Unknown to the crew, the Coast Guard had ceased guarding
the passage of ships great and small
to the rocks and cliffs of Bligh's Reef,
leaving them to wander the hidden dangers
with dangerous innocence.
When the oil finally washed ashore,
the equipment and personnel just weren't there
to clean the spill with proper care.

The seabirds died in greatest numbers.
A quarter million stained the shore,
coated with oil,
wings heavy with tar to flap no more.

The sea otters were next,
diving for their last abalone in a desperate mood.
The rocks they used for dining room tables
were too sticky to rest
on furry bellies now tangled with crude.

The non-human victims formed a gruesome list
that tallied the dead with a vicious twist.
River otters, harbor seals, eagles and orcas
now hunted salmon in final dreams,
and died by the hundreds in oily sheens.

The *EXXON VALDEZ* was not the first disaster,
or the last.
Ships run aground and stain the beaches
with lingering mire.
Oil wells blow, and burn for days in pillars of fire.

Birds and fish and wildlife die,
while corporate heads face cameras and lie.
And Congress lacks the will and tools
to save oceans doomed by ships of fools.

WHEN THE SUN
EATS THE SKY

A bullet of news
lost in blasts from Iraq,
a small paragraph with a thunderous warning:
"Frog extinctions may confirm global warming!"

A verdant rainforest where the sun hardly shines
would seem a strange place to look for signs
that frogs and birds and animals die
when the earth heats up and the sun eats the sky.

In the gray-misted forests a fungus has spread,
and dozens of frog species are turning up dead.
As the sea and air surface temperatures rise,
the fate of the frogs may mean global demise.

Politicians laugh,
call it "pie in the sky"
that the earth heats up,
and the sun eats the sky.

But the littlest beings have added their voice
to such drumbeats of doom,
we may not have a choice.
If we listen and learn,
we can still change our ways,
otherwise our behavior will number our days.

The once-mighty glaciers retreat every day,
and polar bears starve as their homes melt away.
The season of hurricanes never stops storming,
while the vast ozone hole confirms global warming.

As the frogs disappear and the rivers run dry,
the forests burn up and whole species will die,
and those of us left will hear Nature's last cry
as the earth overheats and the sun eats the sky.

Henry Howard. is proud to call himself a poet, because poetry is a form of communicating in the language of the heart. He has been writing in this genre since 2012, and has had the good fortune to have two volumes of peace and justice poetry produced by VAGABOND, in 2014 and 2018. The former won a silver medal in 2016 from Living Now Book Awards, for "Sing to Me of My Rights," his first collection of human rights poems. He is also an activist, and his peace work has been at the heart of everything he's attempted to accomplish in his life. He considers poetry to be a form of activism as well as literature, because it reaches the masses, and carries its own banners that may influence millions to rise up and make the world better!

Henry Howard

THE WALL IS GOING TO GET BUILT

A wall cannot have just one
      side but it can exist in air.

A wall of TVs in a department
      store can tell every kind of story.

A wall can be commissioned
      by cries and mortared by lies.

A wall was once built to save China
      from aliens and Matt Damon in a ponytail.

A wall as tiny as a phone can stop
      a parent from getting to know a child.

A wall cannot be built that will resurrect
      sock hops and communists on trial.

A wall of Lincoln logs can teleport me
      to when I constructed cowboy fairy tales.

A wall is not a room to rest our fears,
      not a heart with four chambers.

A wall can crumble a nation
      even if one or the other is strong.

Martin Ott has published eight books of poetry and fiction, most recently *Lessons in Camouflage*, C&R Press, 2018. His first two poetry collections won the De Novo and Sandeen Prizes. His work has appeared in more than two hundred magazines and fifteen anthologies.

Martin Ott

WORK IN PROGRESS

LAVORI IN CORSO

Work in progress
yawn protruding covers
a voice a saxophone
tar smoke.
The radio scans delays.

The engine exhales
osmosis meat-cement
the jacket flaps its wings like a babble,
like an ancient call without whitheness.
Day TwoDotZero
shatters its light in corners
where no vacuum cleaner arrives
shadows of desks with gadget on walls.

You can't answer, you don't hear
sad monkey
with lost eyes
behind windows with curtains.

Lavori in corso
sbadigliano chiusini sporgenti
una voce un sassofono
fumo catrame.
La radio scandisce ritardi.

Il motore esala
osmosi carne-cemento
la giacca sbatte le ali come un balbettio,
come un richiamo antico senza più candore.
Giorno due punto zero
frantuma la sua luce in angoli
dove non giunge aspirapolvere
ombre di scrivanie con gadget su muri.

Non riesci a risponderti, non senti
primate triste
dagli occhi persi
dietro finestre con tende.

Maria Elena Danelli. I'm from Navigli in Milano, spending my days between painting and poetry, installations and publishing. Theatrical scenographer, graduated in Brera, I worked for almost thirty years at the "Scenografia Ercole Sormani" in Milano, for Theaters all over the world and film sets. My poems and drawings are in some plaquette's editor Alberto Casiraghy named *PulcinoElefante*. I'm in poetic anthologies, including *Novecento no more - Towards the Terminal Realism* by publisher, "La vita felice", Milano and *RISE* by VAGABOND, Los Angeles, 2017. I've read at the historic Bocca Library in Milano, and the monologue in which I interpreted *The Rape* by Franca Rame. I started an editorial and artistic project with Gaetano Blaiotta, the "GaEle Edizioni", which also became "Associazione GaEle". With my left hand I created drawings for a text by Sandro Sardella and a suite by Danilo Blaiotta with GaEle Edizioni dedicated to Jack Hirschman.

Maria Elena Daneli

LA BELLEZA EXISTE

I

La belleza existe
Viene y te destruye
Y sólo la reconoces
Entre el estrago
Y las apiladas ruinas
Entre la noche
Que te parió
El día en que fuiste
Entre tu corazón de niño
O aún muy joven
Y lo que has venido a ser
Una suerte de autómata
De viento entre más viento

II

La belleza existe
En miles de lenguas
Y es políglota
Y es fiel
Y desde los pies a la cabeza

Te ve
Y a veces muere
Pero a menudo
Resucita
Y te rescata de lo que
Nos entendemos
(Escribo para entendedores)
Y para transidos de belleza
Y dolor
Y soledad
Y dudas
Y menosprecio
Y anonimato
Y frustración
Y sinsentido
Pero ella viene y va
Pero ha venido

Pedro Granados

BEAUTY EXISTS

I

Beauty exists
It comes and destroys you
And you only recognize it
Between desolation
And the amassed ruins
Between the night
That brought you forth
The day in which you left
Between your child's heart
Or being still very young at heart
And that you have come to be
A fluke of automation
Of wind amidst more wind

II

Beauty exists
In thousands of languages
And it is multilingual
And it is loyal
And from your feet to your head

It sees you
And sometimes dies
But often
It resurrects
And frees you from what
We ourselves understand
(I write for understanding persons)
And for those overcome by beauty
And pain
And solitude
And doubts
And underestimation
And anonymity
And frustration
And absurdity
But beauty comes and goes
But it has come

Translated from Spanish by,
E. A. Quispe and Albert Efraim

Pedro Granados, Lima, Perú, 1955. Ph.D (Hispanic Language and Literatures), Boston University; Master of Arts, Brown University; Profesor de Lengua y Literatura Española, ICI (Madrid); Bachiller en Humanidades, PUC del Perú. Especialista en la obra de César Vallejo. El 2016, con *Trilce/Teatro: guión, personajes y público*, mereció el Prêmio Mario González de la Associação Brasileira de Hispanistas (ABH). Desde el 2014 preside el "Vallejo sin Fronteras Instituto" (VASINFIN).

Pedro Granados

همه باید کفش هامان را بپوشیم

محبوبم،تو را دیدم که کفش های سبزت را می پوشیدی
تا در خیابان با دیگران
سرود دگرگونی سردهی

دگرگونی صحنه هایی که در خیابان‌های جهان می بینیم
با ثروت و شکوه یک طرفه جاده
و چادرهای کهنه آنسوی جاده روی آسفالت سرد

دگرگونی سیستمی که همه چیز را دسته بندی کرد:،
ثروتمند و فقیر
سیاه وسفید
زشت و زیبا
یهودی و مسلمان
شرق و غرب

محبوبم، ادامه بده به پوشیدن کفشهایت
هم اکنون زمانیست که همه باید کفشهامان را بپوشیم
و تمرکزکنیم بر شباهت هامان بعنوان انسان

تمرکز برای نانی بدون خون برای همه
وآرزو برای مرگی طبیعی ونه مردن در خیابانهای
شیکاگو، پاریس و پالمیرا
با تفنگ و بمب و نفرت!

شاید امروز آن دگرگونی دلخواه رانیابیم
اما میتوان امیدوار بود به شکوفایی باغها در آینده
بدون خاکستر شیمیایی برآنها
و رشد کودکانمان بدون ترس از گرسنگی ودیدن جنگ

محبوبم، به پوشیدن کفش هایت ادامه بده
و قدم بگذار بر جاده ای که صدای همه را متحد میکند
اگر نه اینجا ،
در جاده ی دیگری در این جهان بتو می پیوندم!

مهناز بدیهیان

Mahnaz Badihian

WE ALL NEED TO PUT OUR SHOES ON

My love,
I saw you putting on your green shoes,
to join the people on the streets,
chanting for change

To change the Scene on the streets
In this world with wealth and glory on one side
and tents on cold asphalts on the other

To change the way we divide everything:
Poor and Rich
Black and White
Ugly and Beautiful
Jews and Moslem
East and West
Go on put your shoes on, my love.
It is the time we all need to put our shoes on
To focus on our similarities as a human being.
Focus on piece of bread,
with no blood on it for all.
And a wish to die from natural causes,
not on the streets of Chicago, Paris, Palmyra,....
by guns, bombs and hate!

We may not achieve the change we want now,
but we can hope for future
with new gardens without chemical dust,
with children growing with their families
without poverty and witnessing wars.
Keep putting on your shoes, my love
walk on the roads uniting our voices.

If not here,
I will join you on another road,
somewhere in this world!

Mahnaz Badihian is a poet, painter and translator whose work
has been published into several languages worldwide, including
Persian, Italian, French, Turkish, Spanish and Malayalam. Her
work has appeared in many literary magazines including *exiled
ink!* In the United Kingdom, International poetry magazine and in
Marin Poetry Center Anthology amongst others.

Mahnaz Badihian

HOMELESS

to a tear
dwelling in sorrow
i expound
that should fall
from my eye
welling
from the depth
of unknown terror
(crisis of an age)
descending
in one small sphere
of water
displacement
of vision
occurring
without
the support
of why.

Marcy McNally. As I write this intro, Luigi Pirandello's play, *Six Characters in Search of An Author,* comes to mind. The twist is that I am "One Author in Search of Six Publishers." Although passionate about writing my entire life, I am now returning to my creative writing pursuits, and devoting the majority of time to finishing four novels, numerous short stories, poetry projects, and travel articles. I'm excited to return to these endeavors and interacting with other writers who share writing as a passion and desire to polish their craft.

Marcy McNally

FOR THOSE THAT DWELL IN THE THIRD-SPACE

in their sleeping bags
atop steaming sidewalk grates
giant wet larvae

roofless man sits. sings
it makes me wanna holla...
nest of plastic bags

summer fries white skies
men lie in young tree's sparse shade
one has overdosed

7-11,
we begrudge filthy woman
who wins 50 bucks

baseball cap and bra
red and purple spectacle
stare or look away?

three inch finger nails
he sells the clothes we give him
no one fucks with him

feet wrapped in torn gauze
too big Nikes, no laces
jaywalks between cars

man in wheelchair stands
when children pass his pants fall
tells cops – he can't walk

needs his diaper changed
pulls elevator alarm
he knows we must come

Vodka and gangrene
stench clears hallway masks don't work
she wails, "They raped me!"

man appears pregnant
"I haven't drank in a year!"
doctor rolls his eyes

L.A. warmth calls them
they become invisible
they say it's better

Yvonne M. Estrada is a poet and photographer. Her chapbook, *My Name on Top of Yours*, is a crown of sonnets that explores graffiti and includes original photographs. Her poems have recently appeared in *Talking Writing* and *Fourth and Main* and are anthologized in *Wide Awake: Poets of Los Angeles and Beyond* and *Coiled Serpent: Poets Arising from the Cultural Quakes and Shifts of Los Angeles*.

Yvonne M. Estrada

THE CURE

if you want to cure my soul
cut out your mother's tongue, lay it on a slate of gold;
make it speak the slang of the motherland i'll never know,
eradicate this english dialect from my lips,
tattoo the words of my forgotten tribe around my
hips
teach me how to dance away a pain
that's been rooted for centuries

if you want to cure my soul
dive into the oceans
pull me back the bones of my ancestors thrown over board
go back in time, pluck that first slave ship from the open sea
better yet, light it on fire before it sets sail

if you want to cure my soul
show me photos of my great great great grandmother's nose
tell me exactly who i got these high cheekbones from
delve into the pigment of my skin
pull out the gene that slave master laid there

if you want to cure my soul
and all of the above seems impossible
it's because it is

if you want to cure my soul
you can't

Shakirah Peterson is a Los Angeles native, born and raised in
South Central. Writing is her only passion. She began writing at
the age of 7 and is currently working on her first book of poetry.

Shakirah Peterson

GRAIL *for Palestine/Gaza*

A great weight rests on all our tongues
and the barbs around our hearts
make us barricades of silence.

Tell me then, how can I speak to you
if it's not by shouting?

I shout at the hard sky –
I shout into the ear of a low hanging star.

I shout when my heart is withering like black fruit.
Or when other hearts become brutal hammers
of hate and venom.

A bitter knife carves obscenities into my tender stomach
and I want to yell to stones –
"Please, I am bleeding and my wounds are great." –
But alas, the stones are pitiless tonight.

I scream until my voice is filled with hoarse sobs.

So I wait for the wound to heal.
I wait for the lost blood to become a great tree
which is heavy with fruit.
I wait for lost emeralds to be reset in my God's sick crown.

I become a romantic with ten hands
but am not allowed to use one.

Ultimately, the barricades are not dismantled
and the barbs are not pulled free –
The weight is not suspended.

Tell me then, how can I speak to you
if it's not by shouting?
How can my grail of hope once again be filled?

Victor Avila is winner of the Chicano Literary for Poetry. His work
has been widely anthologized and can be found in such collections
as *RISE (an anthology of Power and Unity)* and *The Border Crossed
Us.* He is also the writer and illustrator of the comic book series
Hollywood Ghost Comics. Victor has taught in California public
schools for almost thirty years.

Victor Avila

Is Gaza

Let me tell you
a tragic story in one word –
Gaza

We all knew Grandma
who didn't know her
her words were full of riddles
we didn't understand

She made bread with me
she bought me a dress
I could never pay her back
it was her last day
I still owe her

The girls keep calling
her name
In hopes
that she will come back

If life is just a passage
then age is not an obstacle
for us

This place
looks like a prison
although it is our land

I know
what war means
what blood means

One day, bulldozers
in the morning
break my toys

We hear the sound
of rockets and
We demand:

Clear this mess
we want it all back
it was once filled
with trees.

Youssef Alaoui

Ink Spiral Methuselah

I live so long, I'm alive when dead.

Ink spiral Methuselah smoking fat wads of tobacco marijuana stogies wider than towel rolls

drinking moonshine of my youth

crawling worms overspill the cup.

O the joy

of a world slipping apart.

River jungles stuffed with candelabras hanging low off bird monkey paths under polished glass

vines, hairy chested ingots.

Build my throne tower of undead observation.

War.

A clean scientific theory that

naturally propagates accidental soldiers in its wake.

The passersby.

The bread bearers.

Home returners.

Makes civilians of soldiers. Mush of heart.

The heaping dead need no clothes no food, no smoke, no hurry.

Mouth full of cod and clay

dried stumps, my arms fold forever in pale dust frozen thin mushroom lawns

cover mummy cloth gown reaches stone cubes, interlocking the floor

of a machine gun tank feeds my two stroke umber.

Scrying glass points at cloud swept ruins screeching like a nest of cobra babies.

Youssef Alaoui

Sprawling almond vapor tundra valley

wagging keel obese time ship, hull burst

taking on air behind dullard cliffs

clicking away at amateur third degree rumination.

Hoping to wake in a gown of swords and commit it all to paper for posterity

as if it were

some kind of graceful act

rather than a clumsy protracted murder carried out with busking change

stuffed in a stinking sock

softening the back of a presidential skull behind the locked and rusted dairy queen.

I am invisible to war

an embarrassment to blood.

The bats will never find me here.

Youssef Alaoui-Fdili is an Arab-Latino, born in California. His mother is Colombiana. His father was Moroccan. The Alaoui-Fdilis are originally from Fez. His brothers and aunts and uncles and cousins are today mostly in Casablanca and Rabat. His family and heritage are an endless source of inspiration for his varied, dark, spiritual and carnal writings. He has an MFA in Poetics from New College of California. There, he studied Classical Arabic, Spanish Baroque and Contemporary Moroccan poetry. He is also well versed in the most dour and macabre literature of the 19th Century. His poems have appeared in Exquisite Corpse, 580 Split, Cherry Bleeds, Carcinogenic Poetry, Red Fez, Big Bridge, Dusie Press, and  nominated for a Pushcart at Full of Crow. Youssef is an original creator of the East Bay literary arts festival "Beast Crawl." In 2012 he created Paper Press Books & Associates Publishing Company. This press offers several important books of poetry and one poetry and art compendium. Youssef also serves as an Associate Editor for Big Bridge Press.

WHENCE ART THOU?

– Where you from?
– From Syria.
– From which city in Syria?
– I was born in Daraa and I was brought up in Homs
– I spent my youth in Lattakia
– I blossomed in Baniyas
– I bloomed in Dier al-Zour and I burned in Hama and flared up in Edlib
– Blazed in Qameshli
– Slaughtered in Dariya

– Who are you?
– I am who fear it.
– Who will lock it up
– Who will stock it up
– Who will burned it up

– I am the one who...
makes flower the trees of the heart
when she passes
Mountains kneel to her grandiose
History turns upside down for her
The earth colors for its sun
I am the one
Who yells and screams in the face of the dictator

I am the one who...
will not abide except only in the head of the nobles
And do not know except only the hearts of the heroes
I am the one who never compromise and not for sale
I am the bread of life and its milk
My name is
Freedom.

Maram al-Masri

CHILDREN OF FREEDOM

Children of freedom
Don't wear their clothes
From the White Company
Their skin has become accustomed
To harsh material

The children of freedom
Wear second hand clothes
Their shoes are sizes too big
To fit for coming year
And often they wear
Only their nudity and scars

Children of freedom
Don't know the taste of bananas
Or strawberries
And don't eat chocolate biscuits
Only dry bread dunked in
The water of patience

In the evening
The children of freedom do not take a warm bath
And don't play with the colored balls of soap
They play with rubber tires
And tin boxes
And the remnants of bombs

Before sleeping
The children of freedom
Do not brush their teeth
And don't listen to stories of princes and princesses
They only hear the silence of cold and fear
On the pavements
In refugee camps
Or in graves
Like all children
The children of freedom
Await their dear mother

Maram al-Masri, a Franco-Syrian contemporary poet and writer, was born in Lattakia-Syria and moved to France in 1982 following the completion of English Literature studies at Damascus University. Today Maram is completely dedicated to poetry, writing and translation. She is considered one of the most renowned, influential and captivating feminine voices of her generation.

Maram al-Masri

LETTER FROM SYRIA

My friend,
One completely plain morning
While drinking tea and carelessly reading the newspaper
The dogs of war knocked on my door

From that moment on there are no newspapers
No bread, no tea on my desk anymore
The laughter of my children is gone

Now
In the middle of the chaos we are constantly trying to find
New survival tactics

Here –
    Death steadily increase
There –
    Heartless politicians
    And academics bury their heads in the sand.

Enesa Mahmić

SUNDAY LUNCH IN EXILE

We didn't talk about our suffering
We taught our children patience
Mastering the silent endurance
Our masters said:
Unnecessary sorrows hijack the glory of God
So, we ate the crumbs from their table
Without any complaint.
We comforted ourselves: *I'm fine. It's ok.*

Tomorrow will be the same,
The concept of discrimination repeats itself.
Gentlemen from social institutions will remind me again
That I'm just a number in the system.
I will be thinking again
How I should leave everything.
Maybe move to another city, another country.
I comforted myself with the illusion of love,
Understanding and forgetfulness
But deep in my heart I knew
There is no country for immigrants.

Enesa Mahmić (1989) is an Bosnian travel writer, poetess and feminist. Her work has appeared in many journals including *Words and Worlds Magazine, Dubai Poetics, Balkan Literary Herald Sent, Eckermann* and anthologies such as *Social Justice and Intersectional Feminism, University of Victoria (CANADA), Spread poetry, not fear (SLOVENIA), QUEEN Global voices of 21th century female Poets (INDIA), Le Voci della poesia; Immagine & Poesia (ITALY), Writing Politics and Knowledge Production (ZIMBABWE), Wood poets (CROATIA), World for peace, World Institute for Peace (NIGERIA),* and more. She won awards for literature: Gold medal *Neighbour of your shore 2017* as best immigrant poetry, *Ratković's Evenings of Poetry 2016* and *Aladin Lukač Award 2016* for best debut book.

Enesa Mahmić

PROPHET'S VOICE

ZËRI I PROFETIT

Despaired of the views
That appear on my window
I hear voices that echo from
The bottom of the souls
Shrieks of which
Keep me hanging over the ground!

I want to scream
With all my voice
And tell them that:
We live
At the end of the apocalyptic world!

I dëshpëruar nga pamjet
Që shfaqen në dritaren time
Dëgjoj zëra që jehojnë nga thellësi
E shpirtërave
Lemeritjet e tyre më ngrisin pezull
Mbi tokë

Dua të bërtas me tërë zërin
Dhe t'ju tregoj se:
Ne jetojmë
Në përfundim të apokalipsit botëror!

68 **Faruk Buzhala**

ACROSS THE BORDER

ANDEJ KUFIRIT

Persecuted on all sides
with grounded hopes deep in our souls
with the question almost dissolved
on our lips
will we meet again?

Mother brother sisters cousins and friends
The war adds meaning to life
incomparable with anything else

I fled the border that separates
the buzz of war with a false calm
I look forward to doing something
Freedom to leaks out of the sky!

Të përndjekur në të gjitha anët
me shpresat fundosur në thellësi
                        të shpirtit
me pyetjen gati se të tretur
në buzët e vyshkura

athua do të shihemi më

nënë vëlla motra kusherinj miq e shokë
lufta po e shtuaka dëshirën për jetë
të pakrahasueshme me asgjë tjetër

unë i ikur andej kufirit që ndan
gumëzhimën e luftës me
qetësinë e rrejshme
pres duke bërë sehir
liria të na pikë nga qielli

Faruk Buzhala is a well-known poet from Ferizaj, Kosovo . He was born on 9 March 1968 in Pristina. He is the organizer for De Rada, a literary club, and also in Kosovo for 100 Thousand Poets for Change. In addition to poetry, he also writes short stories, essays, literary reviews, travel tales, etc. Faruk Buzhala is an organizer and manager of many events in the city of Ferizaj. He has published four books: *Qeshje Jokeriane* (Jokerian Smile) 1998, *Shtëpia pa rrugë* (House without road) 2009 , *Njeriu me katër hije* (Man with four shadows) 2012 and *Shkëlqim verbërues* (Blinding brilliance) 2015.

Faruk Buzhala

ONCE AGAIN

ANCORA UNA VOLTA

once again
the funeral song
over the cursed earth
the stone-throwing kids
aren't enough
to stop people grouping
in war ranks
thebarbarityof
thepowerfulwar
lordsoftheworld

crumbles history
with explosion of flesh

ancora una volta
il canto funebre
nella terra maledetta
bambini lanciatori di pietre
non sono bastati
a fermare uomini schierati
in assetto di guerra

labarbariedei
signoridellaguerra
potentidelmondo

sbriciola la storia
con esplosioni di carne

Gaetano Blaiotta

70

MEDITERRANIAN

MEDITERRANTE

Tonight I dreamed of walking
on a land without land
and with me, men
who had been denied
the earth
they crying caressed me
the path
and they played with my eyes
color of the sea
they rolled them
like waves
to them that had been also
denied the sea.

Stanotte ho sognato di camminare
su una terra senza terra
e con me, uomini
a cui era stata negata
la terra
piangendo mi accarezzavano
il cammino
e giocavano con i miei occhi
colore del mare
li facevano rotolare
come onde
a loro che era stato
negato anche il mare.

Gaetano Blaiotta, born in Eianina-Frascineto (1957). Poetic-theatrical Performer, is mainly involved in writing, drawing, painting and music. Promoter of the traveling group "Disegno Sogno" and of the "Doppio Misto" exhibition, he was in several exhibitions in Italy and overseas. He published poems and drawings in plaquettes "Pulcino Elefante" by publisher Alberto Casiraghy and the books of poems "Contrappunti, Notes on travel on the pedals", "Due", "Mediterrante". His poems have been translated into various languages, also by Jack Hirschman. With Stefania Vecchi he started a publishing project for art folders. Important are the collaborations and attended Ibrahim Kodra and Ernesto Treccani art studios. Since the 90s he meets theater with Federico Grasso and in 2013 with the Nobel Prize winner Dario Fo and Franca Rame. With M. Elena Danelli has undertaken exhibition and publishing projects, creating "GaEle Edizioni" and the Design Gallery in the Small Court in Valcuvia.

Gaetano Blaiotta

71

IMAGINE [THIS]

Tell me, O Muse, your new dystopian tale...

Imagine walking down a city street and running into
a puma chasing its prey
[we've stolen away their wilderness.]

Imagine a puzzled seal decrypting graffiti on the
coral reef
[writers of the Ocean are the new frontier.]

Imagine a wolf eating from a heap in a technicolored
landfill
[the woods have turned into the new waste land.]

Imagine a stag with his antlers on fire
[and no fire department for miles.]
–
Imagine a polar bear playing soccer with your
very skull
[facing extinction is the order of the day somewhere.]

Imagine the new Great Flood coming and
there's no Ark –

[don't cry for salvation – ask yourself what you
could have done to prevent it] –

& get yourself a good pair of oars and a raft.
[Time is running out.]

Freely inspired by artist Josh Keyes' works.

Alessandra Bava is a poet and a translator from the Eternal city.
Her work has appeared in magazines and anthologies both in Italy and in the States. She is
part of Rome's RPB. She has edited and translated into Italian the upcoming *Anthology of
Contemporary American Women Poets* that includes work by Nikky Finney, Joy Harjo, Patricia
Smith and many others. She is busy writing the biography of poet Jack Hirschman.

Alessandra Bava

73

NEVER SEA SERPENTS I SUPPOSE

One day,
We are walking on a beach,
The clouds suggestive of whales.
Apropos of nothing
I suppose,
Though I have been wrong
About sundries assortments
Along the path of this life.
But the beach remains itself
No matter how many political suicides
One observes sailing south.

It can be said without hyperbole
The ocean has offered eons
Of viewing pleasure,
Disasters and masters of nothing,
Species come and gone,
Seldom repeating.
Obviously this goes for us
As well.

I have to wonder at the roar,
The maelstroms and malcontents,
Head cocked to catch the final whimsy,
Sails full and fallow,

Some have lived inside whales
With no ill effect,
Though they are easy to doubt.

Whether the weather will keep an eye out
For us
Is dubious.
And then it is the next day,
And the next,
And the fog whispers I love you,
And no amount of dreaming
Will bring back sea serpents,
Instead the sea seems to possess
Tsunamis seeking take-out.

We keep checking the clouds
But see no incoming messages,
Bottled or otherwise.
It feels proper to wonder
How the tide gets so ripped.
Inebriated on ancient kelp,
How will we ever know
When we've gone too far?
When we've ceased holding care?

Notty Bumbo is a writer, artist, and poet living in Fort Bragg, California. He has been published in a number of small journals and presses, including the Amphigoric Sauce Factory, Words Without Walls, Poesis, Telling Our Stories Press, Peacock Journal, and Calabash Cadence' Taisgeadan, Word Fountain, Poetry South and others. His novella, Tyrian Dreams, is available through Kindle via Amazon Publishing.

Notty Bumbo

THE DUMB

We are struck by that blasts in the roots,

the wood's made dumb with tumors.

The force that calls

the forest and the skies to explode. The small hand that drained our breath;
can't tell yesterday from today we are dumb to grow wise.
Felled villages go the same crooked way

These dumb hacks beauty to freezing fever;

withers blood; and wilts the mouthing rivers
Turns the mountain spring to crude wax.
we are dumb to see our breath burn like

a wild fire burns a forest in the harmattan

The same dumb rules by an untidy name.

The commotions stir the blowing wind;

pulls out strength from our lips;

pain forms and gathers whatever is left

Whatever it is.

Ayo Ayoola-Amale, is of African heritage. Her work as a poet receives critical attention internationally. She is the Muse of Poetic Harmony for Africa and is acknowledged as a poet for positive social change. Ayo enjoys going into schools as a committed advocate of poetry who has seen the critical role that poetry plays as an important catalyst for learning, stimulating creativity and in developing vital communities she believes that poetry should be made a part of students' daily lives. Her poems and other literary works have appeared in several international and national anthologies, magazines and journals.

Ayo Ayoola-Amale

75

Nature Morte

Hölderlin con su arrebato visionario / dijo que los bosques acabarían siendo una pila de leña muerta / la desconfianza hacia los efectos perversos de la modernidad / y la falacia de un progreso con único sentido persiste tanto en el cinismo / del simulacro mediático global / como en la visión apocalíptica de religiones antiguas sin fecha de caducidad / la deforestación indiscriminada en las selvas del Brasil / y la extorsión de minerales en el Congo / demuestran a duras penas que el mayor problema a resolver por la humanidad / sigue siendo la propiedad privada

Hölderlin with his visionary outburst / said that the forests would end up being a pile of dead wood / mistrust of the perverse effects of modernity / and the fallacy of a progress with only one sense persists both in the cynicism / of the global media simulation / and in the apocalyptic vision of ancient religions with no expiration date / the indiscriminate deforestation in the forests of Brazil / and the extortion of minerals in the Congo / are barely showing that the biggest problem to be solved by humanity / is still private property

Samir Delgado Poeta nacido en Islas Canarias (1978), residente en México. Ha publicado libros de poesia y ensayo, es director del Tren de los poetas y ha participado en festivales internacionales en Europa, Latinoamérica, Estados Unidos y Oriente Medio.

Poet born in the Canary Islands (1978) resident in Mexico. He has published poetry and essay books, is director of the Train of the Poets and has participated in international festivals in Europe, Latin America, the United States and the Middle East.

Samir Delgado

Se Llama Poesía

Homenaje a Aldo Pellegrini

Se llama poesía todo aquello que cierra la puerta a los imbéciles, sí.
Todo aquello que abre, en cambio,
la visión y el secreto del mundo a los inocentes,
a aquellos que lo apuestan todo a nada,
los que no guardan, no se cuidan, no acechan,
no calculan y sin embargo están siempre a punto de encontrar
como por casualidad incluso el amor, la muerte, la vida misma.

Se llama poesía todo aquello que tira los pies
tras lo imposible. Lo que revela el otro lado de las cosas,
lo que canta al final del desastre sin motivo alguno.
Lo que te avienta inclemente fuera de tu ser
o invade en silencio – marea extraña –
el interior hasta ahogarte los ojos.

Se llama poesía todo aquello que estalla de golpe en la palabra,
sin aviso y sin lógica. Lo que no puede explicarse
propiamente a los listos, a los que siempre tienen la razón.

Se llama poesía todo aquello que vuelve luego del exilio,
la derrota, los miedos. La luz que un día retorna a los cuartos cerrados
de la vieja memoria; la antigua, recuperada simplicidad de los días.
El viento que reaviva una llama en la noche. Lo que nos sobrevive,
lo que siempre nos queda más acá de la herida, la pérdida más honda,
como una última, callada, oculta fortaleza.

Pedro Arturo Estrada

CALLED POETRY

In honour of Aldo Pellegrini

Called poetry is everything that closes the door on fools, yes.
Everything, on the other hand, that opens
the world's vision and secret to the innocent,
to those who stake all on nothing,
those who don't hoard, don't look after themselves, don't lie in wait
or calculate, and still are always on the verge of finding
as if by mere chance love, death, life itself even.

Called poetry is everything that pulls our feet
after the impossible. That which reveals the other side of things,
and sings at the end of disaster for no reason.
That which mercilessly blows you outside your being
or silently invades – an alien tide –
the inside until drowning your eyes.

Called poetry is everything that suddenly bursts in the word,
without warning and without logic. That which cannot be explained
properly to the smart, to those who are always right.

Called poetry is everything that comes back after exile,
defeat, the fears. The light that one day returns to the closed rooms
of old memory: the ancient, recovered simplicity of days.
The wind that revives a flame in the night. What survives us,
what always remains to us this side of the wound, the deepest loss,
like an ultimate, silent, hidden strength.

Pedro Arturo Estrada – Colombia – 1956. His publications include: *Poemas en blanco y negro* (Editorial Universidad de Antioquia,1994); *Fatum* (Colección Autores Antioqueños 2000); *Oscura edad y otros poemas* (Universidad Nacional de Colombia, 2006); *Suma del tiempo* (Universidad Externado de Colombia, 2009); *Des/historias* (2012); *Poemas de Otra/parte* (2012); *Locus Solus* (Sílaba editores, 2013); *Blanco y Negro, nueva selección de textos* (NY, 2014); *Monodia* (NY, 2015) y *Canción tardía* (NY, 2016). Es premio nacional *Ciro Mendía* en 2004, *Sueños de Luciano Pulgar* en 2007, *Beca de creación Alcaldía de Medellín*, 2012 y *Casa Silva*, 2013, and more.

Pedro Arturo Estrada

Found Poem, or
(Pipe)Lines Composed a Few Miles above Tintern Abbey, on Revisiting Wordsworth during the Signing of the Paris Agreement at the U.N., April 22, 2016

I've never found a poem before
so I went looking. I went looking in my head, and
I found this poem in the things I've been reading lately
about the state of the future.
The state our children are moving into
to live forever more.
The state where they want to burn every bit of fuel in the ground –
green devolution / profit demotive:
Exxon's January 2016 report stating that
"We expect oil, natural gas, and coal to continue to meet
about 80% of global demand"
despite our need to be carbon-free by mid-century
to keep global warming down to two degrees Celsius

I went inside my head and these are some of the things I found on April 22, 2016:
Wen Stephenson, author of *What We're Fighting for Now Is Each Other*, saying
"When are we going to start acting like the science is real?"
and then at the civil disobedience training, where somebody said
"We don't have to know all the facts – it's just profound common sense
to invest in the clean energy industry"
(H.2851: An Act to promote offshore wind energy)
(H.2881: An Act to promote energy diversity – but not Section 13, which asks us to pay a
tariff to subsidize the building of natural gas pipelines).

There is a profound common sense
in the idea of not forcing people to pay a tariff for pipelines
that the most powerful and richest companies in the world
want to use to triple their profits
by selling natural gas on the international markets
(H.2494: An Act Relative to Consumer Protection With Regard to Pipeline Tariffs)

Richard Smyth

79

There is a profound common sense in fixing gas leaks coming from existing gas lines before
building more!
(H.2870: An Act relative to protecting consumers of gas and electricity from paying for
leaked and unaccounted for gas)

There is a profound common sense in fixing leaks when roads are opened up for other repairs
(H. 2871: An act relative to gas leak repairs during road projects)

The omnibus energy bill currently being debated in the MA state house:
Do you know who your representative is?
When's the last time you called? Does she or he know you by name?
Would they recognize you if you saw them?
Have you been to their office yet? Met their assistants?

There is a profound common sense in resisting the building of more pipelines
and so tomorrow morning 9AM West Roxbury Draper Park
hundreds will gather and some will risk arrest
and one will be my son
who will be inheriting the earth,
the burning earth

What will you tell your grandchildren about what you did to stop it?

I'm sorry if this is boring, people.
This is a found poem, after all, and
this is what I find when I go inside my head these days.

Yesterday, shopping for hybrid cars at Jaffarian Toyota, the manager says,
"Gas prices are down, nobody wants to buy hybrids,
I'll sell you this Prius C for a $600 loss because
I pay interest the longer it sits on the lot
and this one's hitting the 60 day mark"

common sense: the abolition of the fossil fuel industry
common sense: building fossil fuel infrastructure is immoral
and like I said at the DPU public hearing last week in Dracut
where Kinder-Morgan pipeline company was seeking eminent domain
to survey people's properties *without their consent*
– this before they canceled the project just yesterday, saying

"It did not have enough business to justify moving ahead with the project" – I said:
"It's a crime against humanity, the future of humanity,
my sons, my grandsons, all our grandchildren.
Common sense vs. uncommon cents:
natural gas sells at 3-4 times the market value on the international market

and the Plotinus quote that hung in my classroom 25 years ago:
"Knowledge, if it does not determine action, is dead to us."

So when are we going to start acting as if we believe that the science is real?

Today the Paris Agreement is signed, but Naomi Klein in today's *Globe:* "Add up all the emissions-reduction plans brought by governments to Paris and it puts us on a pathway to warming the planet not by 1.5-2 degrees Celsius, but by 3-4 degrees, according to many analysts…" In essence, then, our governments said to the world: "We know what we need to do in order to keep us all safe – and we are willing to do roughly half that…."

We are playing with matches
as the world burns.

I found this poem in my head
in the stuff I've been learning lately
about the state of the future,
the state our kids are moving to.
What are the things they carry?
The mark of Cain, for one –
the sins of the Fathers:
asthma, and rashes from fracking fields
and 900 earthquakes per year where there were only one or two:
"Most geologists connect the spike in earthquakes to the state's oil and gas industry –
and its disposal of massive amounts of water into underground caverns.
– faultlines dormant for 300 million years
now waking like Godzilla to shake the earth in Oklahoma:
ignorance – the ignoring and denial – written on the body.

Today on NPR, former Mayor of New York Michael Bloomberg commenting on Republican candidates running for president and their denial of climate science:
"I'm not sure if duplicity or ignorance is better, but it's one or the other."

This is an experiment for me – not scientific.
I've never written a found poem before.
A lot of art is boring because it's an experiment.
This is an experiment in going inside my head.

So I open the door to my head and step in. This is what I see:

my guilt
(I burn fossiil fuel. Every week I fill my tank. I take long, hot showers. We rarely turn off
the light in our basement…)

my fear
(what difference can I make? How can I take on giant corporations and incumbent
politicians? Will I be judged harshly by my descendants?)

my anger
(we've known about this for decades; the fossil fuel industry hired the same "merchants of
doubt" as the ones employed by the tobacco industry: don't they have children and
grandchildren of their own?)

my frustration
(how can people deny the science? "It's only chemistry" my friend Brent once said: light
passes through the atmosphere, but on its way back after bouncing off the earth, the longer
infrared wavelength can't get through the CO_2, so the heat is trapped like in greenhouse.)
(how can people deny the science? 310 parts per million (ppm) carbon in the atmosphere
scientifically measured in 1956; 408 ppm measured as of last week. 350.org is named
after the goal of 350ppm.)
(how can people deny that we're the cause of excess CO_2 gas in the atmosphere? Numbers
based on direct observation: 35.9 billion tons of CO_2 produced by burning of coal, oil, and
gas, plus or minus a small variance. Land use changes added another 3.3 billion tons of
the gas per year over the last decade, though here the uncertainty is larger – plus or
minus 1.8 billion tons.

Found this in the *Boston Globe* last week. I read it: it's in my head: "These three facts:
Atmospheric carbon dioxide regulates temperature at the earth's surface, its levels have
been and are continuing to rise, and human beings are behind that increase – lead directly
to a simple conclusion. All else being equal, human action is driving a global process that
will create and likely already is leading to a warmer world.

Sorry, people: boring, right? Facts and figures, legislative bill numbers. Scientific data. "That's not a poem," you might be thinking.

It's not. It's a FOUND poem. The one I found in my head, just today.

What about Wordsworth? Let me end with his words:

> "And I have felt
> A presence that disturbs me with the joy
> Of elevated thoughts; a sense sublime
> Of something far more deeply interfused,
> Whose dwelling is the light of setting suns,
> And the round ocean and the living air,
> And the blue sky, and in the mind of man;
> A motion and a spirit, that impels
> All thinking things, all objects of all thought,
> And rolls through all things. Therefore am I still
> A lover of the meadows and the woods,
> And mountains; and of all that we behold
> From this green earth; of all the mighty world
> Of eye, and ear, – both what they half create,
> And what perceive; well pleased to recognise
> In nature and the language of the sense,
> The anchor of my purest thoughts, the nurse,
> The guide, the guardian of my heart, and soul
> Of all my moral being.

 **Richard Smyth** earned his Ph.D. in English from the University of Florida in 1994. He has worked in education ever since, first as an Assistant Professor of English at Hamline University in St. Paul, MN, then as a Library Media Specialist and Technology Coordinator at Cathedral High School in Boston, and currently as a Computer Science teacher in Stoneham Public Schools. He is publisher and editor of the environmental poetry journal *Albatross*, now in its 33rd year, and his poems have appeared in print in *Southern Poetry Review*, *Tampa Review*, *Kansas Quarterly*, *Midwest Quarterly*, *Wisconsin Review*, *Southern Florida Poetry Review*, *Florida Review*, and online at *Best Poem*, and poems2go. He also hosts a cable-access TV talk show called *Grass Seeds*, which addresses issues of social, economic and environmental justice (available at http://bit.ly/grass_seeds).

ELEGY FOR THE DEEP EARTH

You fall upon me like an untimely omen
of rebirth of the reef and its resonant clamor
of a distant and banished continent of earth
that some dissolute wanderer has forgotten
a crater of stalagmites snow never tread upon
the landscape chewed to death remains
in the eye of the blind one who has gone mad.

One must destroy this planet
kill the sea
hunt the whale.

Poor terrestrial man.
Your heartless impulse pushes you to death.

My nakedness takes on the warm color of the sun
and its continual blazing.

My beloved, deep earth
constellation of parrots astronauts
with the perennial moon of all your tides
I bury insanity.

My earth
maker of all living things
someone must hail the epic of your
rocky hardness.

Permit me, human shell that I am,
full of the sea,
to tell you: I drink from you eternity and I exist.

Simón Zavala Guzmán

ELEGIA PARA LA TIERRA PROFUNDA

Caes en mí como una intempestiva clave
del renacer del arrecife y su clamor sonoro
de un lejano y desterrado continente de tierra
que algún itinerante disipado ha olvidado
cráter de estalagmitas nieve jamás hollada
el paisaje ultimado a dentelladas se queda
en el ojo del ciego que se ha vuelto demente.

Hay que destruir este planeta
matar al mar
cazar a la ballena.

Pobre hombre terrícola.
Tu desalmado impulso te empuja hacia la muerte.

Mi desnudez asume el cálido color del sol
y sus destellos permanentes.

Adorada mía, tierra profunda
constelación de papagayos astronautas
con la luna de todas tus mareas
entierro la locura.

Tierra mía
hacedora de todas las cosas de la vida
alguien tiene que saludar la épica de tus
pedernales.

Déjame entonces que yo humano caracol
lleno de mar
te diga: bebo de ti la eternidad y existo.

Simón Zavala Guzmán. Guayaquil. Ecuador. Graduate in public and social sciences. Lawyer. Doctor in jurisprudence. Post-degrees in international law and diplomacy; in business administration and in cultural cooperation with emphasis on cultural management. Specialized studies in various fields of law. Author of twenty books of poetry and five books with authors from Ecuador and Latin America. He has obtained, among several distinctions, the Latin American poetry prize, foundation of Buenos Aires, Argentina; the international prize in 2007, Montevideo, Uruguay, and the first mention of honor, in the Latin American poetry competition, of the Editorial Zanún, Buenos Aires, Argentina, 2010. His work has appeared in important publications in Ecuador, Europe, Asia, the United States and Latin America. His books have been published in Ecuador, Peru, Chile, Argentina, Uruguay and United States. Almost all of his poetry has been translated into English and many of his poems have been translated into French, Italian, German, Portuguese, Romanian, Arabic and Hebrew. He has been president of the writers society of Ecuador, Secretary General of the Ecuadorian Culture Council and judge of the constitutional court of Ecuador.

Simón Zavala Guzmán

SOWING SEEDS

I once was a lonely lad
I felt so sad
Alone and on my own
But I have grown
Eden
Endless fields of green
Has been
Polluted with sin
And I, the world, at such a loss
Mother Nature hung on her cross
I chose to resist
Through the vows of the pacifist
To answer the call
By loving all
Even the wicked and cruel
Call me the fool
Say I am naïve

But in Love I do believe
For no man is my enemy
Only what is thought
Needs to be fought
Don't you see?
Saul of Tarsus
On the Road to Damascus
Hear what I say
Sometimes we must go blind
In order to find
Our way
Understand
I will never bloody my hand
For opium and oil
Rather I shall toil
Meeting others needs
Sowing seeds

John Kaniecki is a poet activist residing in Montclair, New Jersey. John is a full time caregiver for his lovely wife Sylvia from Grenada. John served for eight years as a voluntary missionary for the Church of Christ at Chancellor Avenue in Newark, New Jersey. John being open with his bipolar is an advocate for those fighting the stigma of mental illness. In addition to poetry John writes prose and has books of fantasy, science fiction and horror. John has chronicled his overcoming mental illness in his memoirs "More Than The Madness". John is a dreamer and believes in non violent revolution.

John Kaniecki

BLOOMS

I'm at a precipice.

There's nowhere to go but over,
Nowhere to run but back behind me,
But running backwards will show me nothing but the same scenery.

My own footsteps, still fresh and familiar...
Where I've walked, I've already been complete.
And even if it was messy, the stitch has still been sewn.

No one said life came pre-fitted.
Often too large or too small, too hot or too cold, we have to learn to make it just right.
All those imperfections take shape as lessons,
and all the lessons blossom into blooms.

In growth,
Every flower has its own beauty –
Hideous to some and irresistible to others but a flower nonetheless and ever the more.
We, like flowers, cannot bloom in reverse. Yet we will wilt with cycles.
Yet we will die with cycles. Yet we will always be reborn.

Time is not our enemy, nor is it our friend. It is our child and must be taught.
How quickly my life passes or how slowly it develops, the student's success is in part due
to her teacher.
In part her choices.
In part her destiny.

It is also not up to me to fight this body. The framework or context that shaped my figure –
wide at the top and short at the bottom.
Like a river forms so did my hips.
Like a tree develops so has the perspective of my mind.
And my mother's,
And hers before.

Nicole Nelson

From streams we have all become fjords.
On we will trickle, course, or flow freely…
Small or large, the beauty lies in staying true to the rhythm that is you.

No one else can move or stay still quite like you.
No one else can do this life thing like you do.

In comparison we will all be overwhelmed.
An apple to an orange, all fruit over-ripen untasted on the shelf.
Stuck in limbo between Self-hatred and Self worth,
we amount to more than what's left after taxes or on a table of empty plates in a restaurant.

Our little child Time will not wait for us.
She is here, she is NOW.
Patience is not her forte.

Truth is
I'll never be ready
I'll never be as prepared
As I am right Now.

When that call comes in
When that wind starts blowing
When the voice of destiny says rise to your feet
– Shoes or not –
It's Time to
get up
and walk.

Nicole Nelson is a poet, photographer, filmmaker, and musician.
Through her many modalities, she explores themes related to
her social identities as a Woman and a Woman of Color. She
also explores her connection to all living beings, identifying as a
Human and citizen of Mother Earth. Nicole uses words &
images as tools to help raise her own consciousness and
hopefully help raise the consciousness of others. For the health,
happiness & strength of all People, Everywhere.

Don't Stop

she was warned
she was given
an explanation
nevertheless
she persisted

in other words
she resisted
she insisted upon her rights
from the dead dark knights
of fading dominance

toxic masculinity
calls her little lady
putrid patriarchal patois
dusty dicked deacons of decay
obstructing
dumbfucking
an awakening people
to whom they're repugnant
atavistic density proudly displayed
their every public action
hypocritical charade
their only priority
getting paid

nevertheless
she persisted

Rex Butters

in the face of their ham fisted
illegal censure
a dubious procedural mis-adventure
to prevent her
from calling a racist a racist
small brained
rights reducing runts
attempt to rule us
with their mouth breathing grunts
can't bear to hear
Coretta Scott King's
letter
they hate their betters
attempt to chain with abstract fetters
the Truth of these women
like gnats on a light
blinded by fright
their tiny speck shadows
obscure only their existence
their impotent posturing
only fuels the radiant resistance

the future they fear
is
here

Rex Butters, a longtime SoCal resident, has published journalistic writings and poetry in a number of mediums and platforms since the 1970's.

CEO

Life in the tire factory is certainly interesting
For both the employer and employee
Each stabbing the other in the back
With lethal words and snide actions

Who fucked who and who grassed who up
And other issues that are too stupid to believe
It all happens here at Smith's Tires
The bosses get fat from their slave workers' toils

While the workers resent their masters
Having no choice to work long hours for low pay
A few plan revolution but are too scared to act
So they remain defiant but controlled

Each one of hundreds making car tires
A heavy and monotonous job
One step better than the dole
In a company whose profits are millions

With a CEO who flies a Learjet and drives a Hummer
He eats at the top restaurants
Stays in 6 Star hotels
And soon will be assassinated...

Nick Armbrister, is an English writer living in the Philippines, who writes poetry and fiction stories. Topics include current affairs, history, scifi, erotic and more. I've been writing since 1996 and published as long. I also like aeroplanes, reading, hiking, nature, paganism and alternative music. I don't like politics or nasty people. I collect tattoos and want to learn to tattoo. I also write as Jimmy Boom Semtex.

Nick Armbrister

THE NUMBERS GAME

In the end, it was the numbers that did us in.
They lined us up into military rows
And assigned us all numbers
One after one after one after one....
How many, nobody knows.
You see, it's a numbers game
It's all the same
You're not to blame,
You're not your name
You're your number.
Let me explain how it's done,
And how this game can never be won.

See, there are good numbers and bad numbers
High numbers and sad numbers.
Sometimes high numbers are good and low numbers are bad
And sometimes low numbers are good and high numbers are sad.
It all depends on who is doing the counting.
It's not you or me
Nor the numbers either.
They don't know, they're just numbers after all.
Although...
The numbers do count on each other.
Just not you or me

Because we are never free
Of Big Numbers and small numbers,
Negative numbers and imaginary numbers,
You see, it's a numbers game.
It's all the same
You're not to blame,
You're not your name
You're your number.
Let me explain
How it's done.
And how this game can never be won.

94

Igor Goldkind

Prisoner number...
Credit Score number
GPA number
SAT Number
Zip code number
Blood pressure number
Heart rate number
DOB & TOD numbers
House number
Gas number
Phone number
Electricity number
Room number
Water number
Dog tags number
Social Security number
Bank account number
Table number
Sibling number
Temperature number
Flight number
Apartment number
License number
Vehicle registration number
Alcohol level number
Height, weight and age get numbers

I hear you scream:
"I'm not a number, I'm a human being!!"
Sure you are,
Now take a number.
It's for your own protection
There's safety in numbers.

Numbers can answer all of your questions:
How far, how long, how deep, how high, how many,
How often?
Just not 'how come'?
Anyone can count,
But you can't count on anyone.
See, it's a numbers game
That can't be won
It's a numbers game
It's just how it's done.
It's all the same.
You're not to blame
You're not your name
You're your number.
Now count to ten
And start all over again.

Igor Goldkind, is a native San Diegan is an author, educator and producer of advanced media technology innovations. At the age of 14, Goldkind served as a volunteer Science Fiction Coordinator for the now wildly popular San Diego Comic Con. It was in this capacity that he met Ray Bradbury, whom he asked for advice about becoming a writer. In 2015, his project *IS SHE AVAILABLE?* published by Chameleon broke ground in combining Poetry, Comics, Jazz and Animation. His imminent short story collection *THE VILLAGE OF LIGHT* based in the genre of Speculative Realism is to be published this year as well as his first novel entitled simply, *PLAGUE.*

WHAT KEEPS YOU WHOLE

Keep your eye on what keeps you whole.
Deliberate distraction is everywhere.
Fixer Bannon seeded and planted a white
Supremacist (compliant majority) fascist revolt
Within an illegitimate administration.

Keep your eye on what keeps you whole.
The official public policy narrative
Changed. The non-outlier majority is glimpsing
What was filed away and hidden
From wide media radar.

Keep your eye on what keeps you whole.
Since when is expecting good access to
Basic food, housing, and clean water
Extremist? Social Security? Medicare/Medicaid?
Chains pulled yet?

Keep your eye on what keeps you whole.
This is a time of change and choosing
How and when to let go. You know
The essentials that drive your life. You have
Crafted your voice for years.

Keep your eye on what keeps you whole.
Forget the hipster MC who asks
Does he know you? Are you a somebody?
Forget the workers doling out a cot
And shower. Speak in monosyllables.

Elizabeth Marino

Keep your eye on what keeps you whole.
Sometimes you have to channel
That inner Rosalind Russell.
It's the American Way. If you don't remember her,
Ask your mother.

Keep your eye on what keeps you whole.
And that neighbor, whose gentility reminds you of
Rose navigating the ice floes of the North Atlantic –
But not sharing her door –
Graciously hand over your
Extra bag at the food pantry.

Elizabeth Marino is a Revolutionary Poetry Brigade –
Chicago member. Her work has appeared in *RISE (an
anthology of Power and Unity)* by VAGABOND and the
RPB's "Overthrowing Capitalism" anthologies (vols. II & IV)
among others, Her poems can be found in online and print
journals internationally.

THE POUNDING

The pounding persists
On my awakened mind.
It starts with the morning light
Accusing me of keeping at bay
All the shootings of the young
And the looting of a Nation
Under siege from a tyrant
In all but name,
a Don, a remorseless Mafia Boss
Land lording over us with impunity.

It follows me around all the day
As I earn my daily bread and lose
All feeling for the place I once knew
Which, although not utterly innocent,
At least held out some rays of hope.

But the pounding persists,
Leaving but a smudge of dust
Where certainty once resided.
The curtain of sunset brings out
A frozen sky of distant, dark stars
And a half moon like a Grim Reaper.

Eric Vollmer is the Director of Development of Public Works Improv. He has written and produced more than 450 Reader Theater Cabaret programs, drawing upon the talents of hundreds of writers, musicians, comics and dramatists. He's completed his Master's Degree in Communications at UC San Diego, where he was also an Affiliate of the Institute for Global Conflict and Cooperation Studies. He has also served as a Board Member of the United Nations Association, Los Angeles Chapter – and is currently serving on the Raoul Wallenberg Institute Of Ethics Board of Directors.

Eric Volmer

HACER LA REVOLUCIÓN
MAKE THE REVOLUTION

Hacer la revolución
es un acto de fe en nuestra forma
de ver tocar oler masticar sentir.

Hoy mi cuerpo se mueve
al ritmo de mi pena
y mi pena crece hasta convertirse en muralla
y la muralla explota en el abismo
de las contradicciones
y caigo caigocaigo hasta sentir
que mi cuerpo se puede levantar y resistir
y luchar para seguir siendo
nube pájaro canción beso idea

porque así se construyó este mundo
con nubes pájaros canciones besos ideas
y así seguiremos de pie.

Make the revolution
it is an act of faith in our form
to see to touch to smell to feel.

Today my body moves
to the rhythm of my grief
and my grief grows to become a wall
and the wall explodes in the abyss
of contradictions
and I fall I fall until I feel
that my body can rise and resist
and fight to remain
cloud bird song kiss idea

because this is how this world was built
with clouds birds songs kisses ideas
and so we will continue standing.

Adrián Arias, Peru 1961. His four published poetry books include: *Hábitos* (Ediciones de Los Reyes Rojos, Peru, 1984) winner of honorable mention, Julio Cortazar Prize, Buenos Aires, Argentina 1984. *Sueños y Paranoias* (Ediciones Peisa, Perú 1996), winner of the 1st prize of the Peruvian poetry Biennial APJ, jury: Blanca Varela, Antonio Cisneros, José Watanabe, Washington Delgado, Jaime Urco. *Divine Punishment* (Ediciones Jaime Campodónico, Perú 1999), honorable mention of the Copé de poetry prize, Peru. *26-10-2028* (Ediciones Copé, Petroperú, 2000) winner of the third prize, in the Copé de poetry Biennial, Peru. He has won the prize for best poem of the Poetic Nights of Struga, Macedonia, 2009. His poetry appears in anthologies in Peru, Spain and the United States, as well as a collection of limited special editions of all his platelet poetry readings, two of which have been translated into English by the poet Nina Serrano, a cultural activist on radio in KPFA Berkeley, California.

Adrian Arias

Yo No Salí a las Calles

Tan solo alcancé a susurrar
los cuarenta y tres nombres

No alcancé a gritar de rabia
ni a pintar las paredes
ni a acompañar a nadie
en ese dolor
que tampoco logro sentir

Yo no sé lo que es ser
golpeado y desollado vivo
Destinado a no respirar más
A vagar en el limbo de la pena
buscando mi nombre
y hasta mi cuerpo

La indignación sacude
nos rodea y hace sucumbir
ante lo insensible que es
escribirla a garabato propio
con acentos impropios
y negociaciones mudas

No salí a gritar con tinta
para dejar en sangre
sus nombres tatuados
Los veinte mil nombres
Elevarlos hacia una luz
que no percibo pero ansío
creer en su existencia

Una dimensión amable
Infinita claridad en el espacio
Un lugar nunca soñado
Un poema de fe en algo
más que esta carne
y toda esa sangre derramada
que una vez seca, se olvida

Yo no conozco otra tierra
ni otro cielo
pero lo imagino
porque necesito creerlo
porque necesito crearlo
Un sitio donde el sacrificio
tenga un para qué

Para seguir insistiendo.

Pilar Rodriguez Aranda

I Didn't Go out onto the Streets

I was barely able to whisper
the forty three names

I wasn't able to cry with rage
nor paint the walls
nor accompany anyone
in such pain
which I can't feel either

I don't know what it is
to be beaten and skinned alive
Destined not to breath again
To wander in the limbo of pain
searching for my name
and even my body

Indignation shakes
surrounds and makes us yield
given the insensitivity of
writing it in one's own scrawl
with improper accents
and mute negotiations

I didn't go out to scream in ink
to leave in blood
their names tattooed
The twenty thousand names
Raise them towards a light
I don't perceive yet yearn
to believe in its existence

A kind dimension
Infinite clarity in space
A place never dreamed
A poem about faith on something
more than this flesh
and all that scattered blood
once dried, forgotten

I do not know of any other Earth
nor sky
but I imagine it
because I need to believe
because I need to create it
A place where sacrifice
makes sense

To keep on insisting.

Pilar Rodríguez Aranda currently resides in Tijuana, Mexico. Her poetry has been translated into English, Arabic, Greek, Italian, Portuguese and German. She has published the books *Asunto de mujeres* (2012), and *Insistencia en el sueño* (2018); the placket *Verdes lazos* (2014); the CD *Diálogos de una mujer despierta* (2016), with 12 poems set to original live music; and the eBook *Una familia más/One more family* (2018).

Pilar Rodriguez Aranda

DESTERRADOS

Se estremece la nube preñada,
derrama su grisácea luz
rota por los árboles recién lavados.
Ya el alma no es un rincón de paz,
el destino adquiere
la danzante figura de la maga loca del poema
que aflora en el pecho atormentado.

Candil de perpetuo aceite
baila la lluvia en los tejados,
y embravecen los lagos nacientes
de entre espinas y rosas de eternidad
que taladran el tiempo
y perfuman el dolor.

Pon más aceite en tu candil,
que se llenen los campos de espigas y niños,
voces del aire en canción recién aprendida,
pollerones y perros alborotan la mañana,
incierta mañana que se levanta
lavada y amorosa,
enternecida y lenta,

esparciéndose a retazos en los caminos,
reventando el llano
por el que vamos bebiendo el agua
que brota de los siglos y los sueños.
Saltando, cantando, absorbiendo,
mirándonos a los ojos,
el poema surgiendo entre nosotros,
ave pertinaz y blanca,
como de pureza y de niebla.

Por la noche nos cobijamos bajo las nubes,
encendemos el fuego
y surgen sombras de aquelarre,
visiones de espanto al lado del enrojecido amor.
En la lumbre apasionada de los besos
amamos, construimos, procreamos,
devolvemos a la adversidad insolentes gestos
pues amaneceremos siempre
estirpe, derecho, palabra
con el anhelo visionario sufriendo en la piel
y en el cerebro la mirada del destino.

Danae Brugiati Boussounis

BANISHED

The loaded cloud trembles,
spilling its grayish light
broken by freshly washed trees.
The soul is no longer a hideout of peace,
Fate acquires
the dancing figure of the poem crazy magician
that surfaces in the tormented chest.

Lamp of constant oil
the rain dances on the rooftops,
and rave the nascent lakes
from between thorns and roses of eternity
that drill the time
and perfume the pain.

Put more oil in your candle,
let the fields be filled by children and ears,
voices of the air in a song just learned,
skirts and dogs ruffle the morning,
uncertain morrow that gets up
washed and loving,
tender and slow,

scattering in pieces on the roads,
bursting the plain
in which we go drinking the water
that springs from centuries and dreams.
Jumping, singing, absorbing,
looking into each other's eyes,
the poem emerging among us,
persistent and white bird,
as from purity and fog.

At night we shelter under the clouds,
we light the fire
and shadows of the coven emerge,
visions of fright next to the flushed love.
In the passionate light of kisses
we love, we build, we procreate,
we give back to adversity insolent gestures
as we will always wake up
lineage, law, word
with the visionary longing suffering on the skin
and in the brain, the gaze of destiny.

Danae Brugiati Boussounis

103

Pronuncien Sus Nombres
Speak Their Names

Algunos de los que amo se han ido	Someone I love has gone away
Y la vida no es lo mismo.	and life is not the same.
El mejor regalo que puedes dar	The greatest gift that you can give
sus nombres en un suspiro, unidos al viento.	their name in a breath, added to the wind.
Necesito escuchar las historias	I need to hear the stories
ylos cuentos de los días pasados.	and the tales of days gone past.
Necesito que entiendas	I need for you to understand
que sus palabras deben durar	that their words must last.
No podemos hacer más recuerdos	We cannot make more memories
ya que no están aquí,	since they are no longer here,
por lo tanto cuando me hablas de ellos	so when you speak of them to me
ya no tengo más tristeza, ni lágrimas,	I have no more gloom, no tears,
Solo el sentido de sus sonrisas en el aire.	just the sense of their smile in the air.

Danae Brugiati Boussounis (Panama, 1944) staged the oratorio *AxionEsti* by Mikis Theodorakis in verses of *Odysseus Elitis* (2010) at the National Theater of Panama and organized the Nikos Kazantzakis Week at the University of Panama in September 2017. She has published two storybooks: *Pretexts to Tell You* (Forum / Workshop Sagittarius Editions, Panama 2014 and 2016) and *On the Banks of the Possible* (the duende grammars, Panama 2016) and one of essays: *Luminous Texts* (Editorial Mitosis, Panama 2016). Her stories have been published in magazines such as "Maga" and "Panorama de las Américas" (COPA) and in anthologies: *The Newcomers* (Foro/Taller Ediciones), Panamá, 2013; *Scenarios and Provocations*, Mexico, 2014; *Vida y Muerte*, (Editorial Benma), México 2015 and *Central American Anthology of Micro-stories*, (Índole Editores), El Salvador, 2016. She is preparing a book of essays on Panamanian painters and a collection of poems.

Danae Brugiati Boussounis

POLITICS

Man's politics
is a table with three legs?
It is unsure foundation.
Unfit to hold up our hopes.
It is stitched together with slimy promises.
Forged with all the good intentions a founding father / slave owner could have.
Our nation is filled with those who find allegiance to
Donkeys & Elephants.
Both are stubborn and heavy
Neither willing to budge for the other.
I watch as they fight.
Play musical chairs with senate seats.
Our branches of government are broken and tangled
Watered with self-preservation.
Their political house party is more kindergarten than congress
Arguing whose turn it is to be team captain.
And it's getting so hard to tell them apart.
You see,
they dawn their suits and ties like swords and shields
all competing in a Game of Thrones.
Making Lannister promises to their constituents.
These disloyal knights in shining armor
They will dragon as soon as you let them.
Burn down your futures to further the views of their donors
I ask you.
Be careful where you place your faith
Be accurate where you send you prayers.
Remember,
Man's laws will never be powerful enough to police the human heart.
No.
Just scary enough to make man wear a civilian mask,
pay taxes and BBQ.

Alexander James

105

A Bad Dude

(In Response to the shooting of Terrance Crutcher)

September 16th, 2016
Officer Shelby Bo shot and killed Terrance Crutcher.
Her Husband, watching from police helicopter upon seeing Terrance says,
"That looks like a bad dude".

Alex –
Remember to smile

Alex –
Deflate your chest

Their eyes armed with assumptions &
prejudice makes my skin gunpowder.

Alex –
Wave, Make eye contact

It's as if the sight of a black man
breathing
chokes them with fear.
Make you clinch purse like newborn.
Make wait for the next elevator.

When they see me.
They never
see poet,
see father,
see husband.

No wonder
I must constantly find new ways to disarm myself.
More Carlton less Will.
More WB less BET.

I believe that comply, is a costume stitched together with
Jim Crow & bias. Adorned with shackles and chains.

Here in America,

My biggest threat is being seen as threat.
I am forced to be vigilant.
To watch how you watch.
So interactions with others in the wild must
become petting zoo. Simple. Easy to swallow.
Entertaining.

Alexander James

One day I would love to show you the beauty of the beast in my chest.
How my intelligence can be claw.
Be fang.

But.

Some opportunities, jobs, stages only come
if I look caged.
I feel like
 a dragon who must swallow his flames.
 A muzzled shark.
 A mute lion.
To survive I've had to make strait jackets
out of your assumptions.

My greatest fear is that you will see me
turning a side walk into a runway.
And you will be threatened by my wings.
Your prejudice and ignorance will hold hands like
scissors hungry for feathers
and I will have shove myself back into a cocoon.
Swallow my pride. Pay the cost of my tomorrows, so you can feel
superior I mean safe
today.

All because I want to live.
See my children again, kiss my wife again.

So, I pretend that I fit in your boxes.
Even if it's in a cage of your imagination.

Alexander James I am a native to South Central Los Angeles, raised
by my single mother. I took pride in being the black sheep in most
circles growing up. Now as a Baptist minister, social activist and
youth advocate and fulltime spoken word artist. This mixture of
experiences has helped me carve a unique perspective and delivery
that has awarded me a strong Los Angeles fan base and some
national acknowledgment & many university partnerships.

THE SANTA CROSS ARCANE

1.

Guns and money,
Guns and money.
This isn't about
Dempsey & Tunney.
It's about the religion
of the very unfunny
United States and the
17 dead in Parkland

at the hands of Santa
Cross with that metallic
white supremacist look,
Saint Nikolas Cruz, who
hates Jews, Blacks, and
announced himself as
a future school shooter
even before he pulled

the trigger, (go figger,
niggas and kikes),
it's all about stukas,
lugers and dykes;
it's all about lonely
reclusively angry
adherence to evil
websites, and

2.

you and your more
than 700 military bases
in virtually every country
on earth, your hypocrite

lies, your two-party
game, the shame of one
with the name of the
Capitalist Party.

Hands up! Salute
the dead chief's living
apprentice to the music
of the opportunes that
sound like, "Here you
can do anything to
make a billion, screw
anyone on the way",

massacre at a Vegas
concert or at Florida
schools or schools in
other states as well.
No weeping. Guns
don't cry. They come
from history's slave-
owning arsenals, of

cowboys, homegrown
gangsters, mafia dons;
and we got the 2nd,
we wear the 2nd,
we unfurl the 2nd
like show-offs of
the freedom to buy
an AR-15 blockbuster

Jack Hirschman

as early as 18 years
of age, and there are
Blacks for it as well
because they know
that in this race-sick
society they'll need
self-protection from
the cops, who're

continuously and
on every street,
in every store,
at every opportunity
dissing, frisking
and nixing their
brothers and
sisters galore.

3.

And how ironic the 17
should have been killed
at a high school named
Douglas in Black History
Month, when the words

– for the most part still
unknown and unread –
of Frederick Douglass

underlies the atrocity
committed by a broken
punk nazi sympathizer
who spent his time,
when not shooting off
his loudmouth guns,
coozing with whores,
kinky Hannah & Nina,

on the MLIF website
before going to sleep
with his Trumpy Bear,
dreaming of a Tweet
from the President
himself so he can read
Its secret message
between the heils.

THE VAFANNCULO ARCANE

1.

As men sing men's zonias
and lie like lyres on their sides
beside the rumps of trumpery

grown in size in order to make
the peniseal gland the best
of the band beaters in the hive

of the bogus bees in this very
alphabet soup that clearly and
with jeery slayall mendacities

spells out that, deeper than the
Mafia of the Amalfi coast or the
Ficcolo Porno of No Bich or

the Nosa Costra or the Tamarra
Comorrow, all thighs, even ones
not given to being given the once

over, hang dangling out like flags
of the bourgia that trumpet, to the
song of a terrified world of a sleazy

pack of sheepish, teary eyed men
bah-bah baying: In lies we trussed!
For what fab of a fib of a vafannculo

this age has lowered over our heads,
so that every youth, be it he or she,
has had their future pockets picked

by the swindles of evangels ghoulore
or ratwing denierfiers of every hollow
caustic moment, including the ones

whore've been waiting smentarian
years for the reserection of the limp
dick of the hero of everybaddy's

longed-fur dream of humping Trump
with a doll named Dough for his not
telling the truth when, for hevery work

crew jobbing in the gutter, the robots
have laid off 10,000 men and women
every day in this god hole you ass aye.

2.

And we've all been axed to hiccept the
lies that've humputated the very depths
of what it means to be a mirror's con.

It's lies, it slys, it slies allover inside
our hearts, our arts, our rhythms; it
curses through our ribbers, elevates

the foot to the need of a knee, seeing
Big Ass open his mouth and releasing
more gas than all the stations of the

Jack Hirschman

111

crass that's making America grit a goon.
So save your spittle, inviced in the future
where nevermire tumented, fabulously

gianed to the crass of billionaires, you'll
deal your sleeve a card whose image
will be of yourself dealing cards shilly –

willy at the poker table in Let's Begas,
following who hustles to high heaven
and you get nothing but allout war

served up with the stink of the money
from munitions minted in Mentisy,
amounting to nothing but the lie that

America's told itself for as long as it's
been a slave to that one fat smello
who feels himself smart, and his vice

kick in the pence, hoosier ma, does
she smut? And with the dirt man, the
suckrootaryan Bannonton of feel-smart

fame, it's clear to see and easy to say,
in the neonest glitter of old Broadway,
the whole damned trio smells of fart.

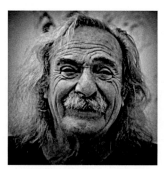

Jack Hirschman is the emeritus communist Poet Laureate of the City
of San Francisco (2006-2009). This year, Swimming with Elephants
Publications of Albuquerque, New Mexico, published his and Idlir Azizaj's
Albanian translations of the Kosovo poet, Jusuf Gërvalla, in A MOTHER'S
BLESSING. He is also archanizing his poems and preparing THE ARCANES
#3, his own masterwork published in the American language in Italy by
Multimedia Edizione in Salerno.

12 Years a Slave

I can't believe the things
we do to ourselves
These machinations and places
We manifest hell
The way we let the hate,
horror, genocide swell
And we crush stories
So those affected never
get a chance to tell
The lash, the chain,
The pain, the whip
The bullet, the slur,
The mind's warped trip
The rope, the noose,
The knot, the slip
One sentence in a chapter
then we silence our lips
History books
Written by former slave-owners
Plantation class
Whole lot bleed for no one
Hearts made of stone
Inside so alone
Take your anger at yourself
Out on the one you own
But no human being
Is another's property

Every man, woman, child
Got a spirit born free
Got a body, got a mind,
God-given abilities
We all entitled
To our shared humanity
Tears running down my face,
From what we constantly run from
And never wanna face
I stare into that darkness
And I feel so disgraced
If we all one people
why we divided by race

Why we do what we do to ourselves
Why we lose what we thought
what we had what we felt
How could man be so cruel and evil
What we got up inside that stays locked
and we keep trying to fill
Why we do what we do to ourselves
How could God make a earth
that gets filled with such hell
What we mean when we say
freedom's real
Take a look at the past
How it lasts
Something we got to feel

Chris Devcich

I can't believe the things
we did to ourselves
The way we treated those
Who were just trying to help
'Til we took advantage of every chance
Killed the tribe after Thanksgiving
Outlawed the Sundance
We all got blood on our hands
Stolen land
Where we stand
Who was killed for what you now have
And I ain't trying to guilt you to death
Imma try and feel that as I breathe deep
and feel the breath
We got to come to grips, come to terms
with what we've done

What has come, what has gone,
Yeah, how the west was won
No treaty made is honored,
Not one,
Every treaty ever made was broken
into a thousand suns,
So if we wish to survive,
Not live,
Just get by,
We cannot turn a blind eye
To the treaties, slaves, beatings,
past bleeding,
Why?
I don't wanna just survive
I wanna live, I wanna thrive

LOSS FOR WORDS

I'm at a loss for words...
Hold Up... I found them...

I'm at a loss for words
The comfort and convenience of illusion has been disturbed
Perturbed,
Unnerved,
When we heard...
The sound of the dropping of a million bombs in one verb
Elected
By a minority of fear
By a system that was relevant when nationhood was near
Mark a box to keep yourself thinking inside it
But we outside it now
Our mental landscape has widened
Not what we wanted
Maybe more what we needed
Regardless of what these out-of-touch, paid-off pundits never heeded
Warning now we all feel the global warming
The sound of hearts beating sound like tears falling down and storming
We torn in
Inside, outside USA
The People and the evil got a long road to unpave
A pipeline pushing poverty and poison
We all sinners now
No matter how much oil anointed
US

Chris Devcich

The U.S., The "In God We Trust"

The godless, the god lust,

The god that's way up in stardust,

Now the People see the face of who and what it truly is

Now maybe they can see the truth of that face staring back in the mirror

This is a call to act

Take a look at your issues back

When they formulated you

In the form of shame, blame, guilt, logic and fact

See it, bleeding in the streets,

In the walls that already exist

Resist

But the hatred will continue to persist

We are Love

The force that rises us all above

The black and white judgment

The grief of police firing slugs

At those who's skin bears the mark of melanin's smudge

Who gave you the right to kill?

Who gave you the right to judge?

Who gave you the right hate?

Mind set and never budge

This is complete and moving, grooving

We flowing like some of these floods

People be strong

Happy, healthy, wealthy, moving as one

We woke with air in our lungs

And the Big Light of the sun

We see this for what it is

No longer can we dismiss

What we had as the luxury of denying what truly exists

They were all red states before any of this

Who knew what it meant to live

While running with the wind

But here we are now

How?

Doesn't matter

It's reigning loud

And we can all hear it screaming our name out in the crowd

So rise up

Take the streets,

Walk on in flowing peace

With your head up...

I know this change it begins in me

Chris Devcich is a human being, who also happens to be a musician, songwriter, MC, poet, DJ, producer, editor, filmmaker and what some call an "activist". He is a Hip Hop artist who performs under the alias Guido Corleone and is a member of the LA-based crew known as the Luminaries. But perhaps more than anything – he is a helper... and part of the ancient warrior society based on nonviolence known as Akicita Heyoka – the Fool Soldiers. Having traveled and toured across the country and various parts of the world, alongside artists ranging from  Dead Prez to The Dead Kennedy's, Chris loves rocking microphones, connecting with people from all over and learning from their culture. He works with folks from a wide range of circles and communities, as part of his strength is walking in and out of these different worlds, connecting the dots, building bridges and tearing down walls of separation. In embracing his own humanness, and channeling it through his art he is finding a way to see all things – and all life – as relative. Doing it for the people, he shines a light into his own darkness to reveal The Truth, as he stands with all of us – in Love and Solidarity.

There's this Poem

There's this poem for you now
wandering around, it's like
it beams in the dark
sparks remarks
parts of speech packed and stacked
vowel to vowel
pleas to howls
chants and rants
proposes, it noses its way
across your skin
and then sings, grows wings,
flings whole words against the wall
until they submit, fit, witness a life,
round rhymes, lined verse, you know
it has hands, makes plans, stands alone
shownshimmerings
of what metaphors can do
and you wait for it
shake for it
hate for it to end.

There's this poem
here, hanging in the air
like a scent of holy Roman candles
or an aroma of bones honed in catacombs
for years composing space
laced ceiling to floor with nouns
knelt in prayer there,
kings' long fingers wearing rings
golden things bringing bejeweled
language to your mouth.

Charlie Becker

There's this poem, see
it has eyes and cries for friends
who died too young, too soon
before they knew what poets can do.
If it takes a village to raise a poet
then I say it takes more poems
to raise us up:
The ones who were oppressed but still spoke the truth,
the ones who wrote in secret, silent journals
or shouted out into empty rooms,
the ones who scribbled on sides of buildings or protest signs
never to know their manifesto unfold,
the ones shot down by guns or AIDS
the ones who were my loves
the ones who hoped to reach landings
turn corners
and find the crystal stair
there
there's this poem

Charlie Becker is a poet and fine artist who brings poetry to
under-served high school students in Los Angeles through
the Living Writers Series (LWS). He has participated in the
Community Literature Initiative (CLI) for the past four
years, and studied poetry and fiction writing at Barnsdall
Art Center in Hollywood for more than ten years. Some of
Charlie's poems have been published by Beginnings
magazine, Quill and Parchment, and Grenadier Press (an
anthology of writings by LGBT-Q seniors called, "My Life is
Poetry"). His first book of poems and drawings, "My Life is
Poetry", was published by World Stage Press in July, 2016.
Charlie lives in West Hollywood, California.

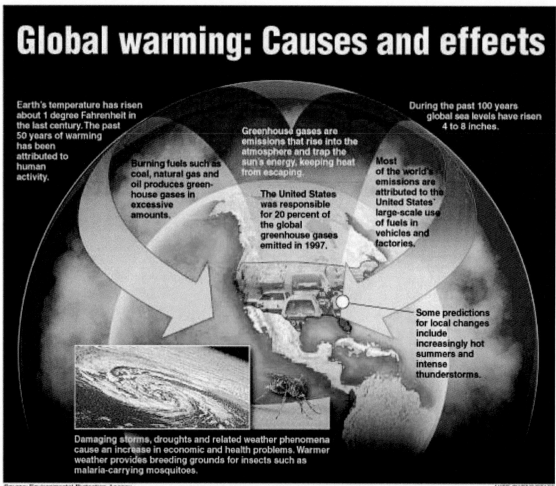

Global warming: Causes and effects

Earth's temperature has risen about 1 degree Fahrenheit in the last century. The past 50 years of warming has been attributed to human activity.

During the past 100 years global sea levels have risen 4 to 8 inches.

Burning fuels such as coal, natural gas and oil produces green-house gases in excessive amounts.

Greenhouse gases are emissions that rise into the atmosphere and trap the sun's energy, keeping heat from escaping.

The United States was responsible for 20 percent of the global greenhouse gases emitted in 1997.

Most of the world's emissions are attributed to the United States' large-scale use of fuels in vehicles and factories.

Some predictions for local changes include increasingly hot summers and intense thunderstorms.

Damaging storms, droughts and related weather phenomena cause an increase in economic and health problems. Warmer weather provides breeding grounds for insects such as malaria-carrying mosquitoes.

Source: Environmental Protection Agency

NATE OWENS/STAFF

120

BAM BAM BANG DISCANT

*"We shall be the melody of a subversive
and innocent chant   that wanes."*
            ~ Alberto Masala

"I only improvise, like everyone else"
            ~ Tom Waits

Don't alight from the marred
heart of desire from feeling the gap
between the human condition and
the music swarming a colored desert
inside a life-movie
with a skimmed deboned sound
from traveling without conquering
from thinking
from dreaming

it happens every day
the tongue is a place
the tongue that hosts me
you walk in and ask where the restroom is
I like the music that lives on the edge
there's who listens to sultry songs
writing feels so strange to me

the most scorching summer of the century is ablaze
it's slipped under my skin
the refrain of the economic recovery blah blah blah
doesn't convince me
I dream of it at night too
hearing it has enchanted and disarmed me

I move forward by images
words boil over
on a road with open doors
a color   a sign   a sound

borders that move
I don't like barbed wire labels
I'm interested in fleeing rustling when
it turns into drops of splendor
as shrilling as Milan's tramway wheels

words leave stains
marks of the evening meal variations on
a dirty tablecloth
a lot of poetry lacks company
you listen to odorless words
umbilical ardors
temperature-controlled words
words lacking migrations lacking movements

Sandro Sardella   121

those keen on outbursts are not looked kindly upon
those who wish to change annoy
jumping the line playing it cool
elbowing and slyness are preferred

too much sea surrounds us
too much compulsive
sky
the story of Dada is rendezvous
              it's burst brain
   it's volcano's lava against war
it's mangled crystal-ware for new cultures
it's the crumbling of gang violence
it's drilling command
it's moving forward

you undress of your many clothes
along this river that flows with indifference
the weather-beaten
dreams burn

to cure emptied words
amid loathsome supermarket music

I open a Cabernet some drops fall to the ground and
we drink a swig from the bottle

I listen to ... I watch ... I walk a step away
the heart is present associating with chaos and
searching for the core

O life!

words connected to the sense of hunger always in lie
burning with urgency immediacy vulnerability
with the shamelessness of dreamers
outside, outside unexpressed cemeteries of desires

somebody who knew a thing or two said "revolutions
are no lunch gala"

the assertive eternal present dictates and fills the void

Tom Waits' shoes with holes
Paolo Conte's Langhe sandals
Jovanotti's danced unlaced heavy-duty boots

poems to keep in the pocket
wild flowers of revolt
of muddy lagoons
of a world turned into a tourist resort
while listening in the dark
surrounded by the silence of the old mill
only the water speaks

out of time you sit with an open
book on your knees
out of time you scribble on a leaf
with a pencil
you're sitting on a bench in a park in Varese
the body in direct sunlight
you dare yawn   do nothing   stay still
indifferent to the productive and consumer frenzy
of everything and all and of all things
in a magma that leaves us unfit
dazzled by the gold dust that upholsters
the greed of masters & servants

on the foreshore joyous sandcastles
enough of rubbish plastic toy

blackbirds and swallows seem to laugh
at my stumbling

in an uphill sea
I've felt your breath within mine
I stole this line leafed through
as a flower to a singer

today is a good day
to scream NO TAV – NO WAR

HOORAY FOR YOUR EYES
I will send you a postcard
as the sun sets beyond the window
on our faces

forgive me she friend if I bug you
with these words filthy of world
if I rub and scratch
your marble floors
your blank page
but it's cold
and my heart still beats
happy and desperate
lyrical and epic

DISCANTO BAM BAM BANG

"Saremo melodia che si allontana
di un canto sovversivo   ed innocente."
~ Alberto Masala

"Mi limito a improvvisare, come tutti"
~ Tom Waits

è vietato scendere dal cuore
infangato dal desiderio di sentire lo scarto
tra la condizione umana e
la musica che invade un deserto a colori
dentro una vita film
con un sonoro scremato disossato
dal viaggiare senza conquistare
dal pensare
dal sognare

ogni giorno succede
la lingua è un luogo
la lingua mi ospita
entri e chiedi dov'è il bagno
a me piace la musica che sta ai margini
c'è chi ascolta canzoni afose
ancora mi fa strano scrivere

infuoca l'estate più calda del secolo
è entrata nella mia pelle
il ritornello della ripresa economica blabla
non mi convince
me la sognavo anche di notte
quel calore mi ha incantato e disarmato

procedo per immagini
ribollono le parole
su una strada con le porte aperte
un colore un segno un suono

frontiere che si spostano
non mi piacciono le etichette filo spinato
mi interessano i fruscii sfuggenti quando
possono divenire gocce di splendore
stridenti come le ruote di un tram di Milano

macchiano le parole
patacche del variare del pranzo serale su
una tovaglia sporca
in molta poesia manca compagnia
senti parole senza odore
ardori ombelicali
parole in temperatura controllata
parole senza migrazioni senza movimenti

Sandro Sardella

125

non si vede di buon occhio chi tenta degli slanci
infastidisce chi desidera cambiare
si preferisce sgomitare furbeggiare
saltare la fila fare finta di niente

troppo il mare che ci circonda
troppo cielo
incontenibile
la storia di Dada è incontro
            è cervello esploso
    è lava di vulcano contro la guerra
è cristalleria massacrata per nuove culture
è sbriciolamento della violenza del branco
è un trapanare il comandare
è andare

ti spogli dei troppi vestiti
lungo questo fiume che scorre indifferente
i sogni bruciano
espongono alle intemperie

curare le parole svuotate
tra lo schifo della musica da supermercato

apro un Cabernet qualche goccia alla terra e
ne beviamo un sorso dalla bottiglia

ascolto ... guardo ... mi allontano di un passo
il cuore c'è tra frequentazione del caos e
ricerca dell'essenza

oh vita!

parole legate al senso di fame sempre lì
a bruciare urgenti immediate vulnerabili
con la spudoratezza necessaria ai sognatori
fuori fuori dai cimiteri dei desideri inespressi

uno che la sapeva lunga diceva che "le rivoluzioni
non sono un pranzo di gala"

l'eterno presente prepotente impone e riempie il vuoto

le scarpe bucate di Tom Waits
i sandali langhe di Paolo Conte
gli anfibi slacciati ballati di Jovanotti

poesie da tenere in tasca
fiori selvaggi in rivolta
dalle lagune limacciose
di in mondo villaggio turistico
fare degli ascolti al buio
attorno al silenzio del vecchio mulino
solo l'acqua parla

fuori tempo stai seduto con un libro
aperto sulle ginocchia
fuori tempo scarabocchi su un foglio
con una matita
stai su una panchina in un parco di Varese
il corpo sotto la luce del sole
osi sbadigliare   far niente   star fermo
assente dalla frenesia produttiva e consumistica
di tutto e di tutti e di tutte cose
in un magma che ci lascia incapaci
abbagliati dalla polvere d'oro che riveste
l'avarizia di padroni & servi

sul bagnasciuga gioiosi castelli di sabbia
basta giochi di plastica pattumiera

i merli e le rondini sembrano ridere
del mio sbandare

in un mare in salita
ho sentito il tuo respiro dentro il mio
questo verso sfogliato come un fiore
l'ho rubato a un cantante

oggi è una bella giornata
per gridare NO TAV – NO WAR

W I TUOI OCCHI
ti manderò una cartolina
mentre il sole oltre la finestra tramonta
sui nostri visi

scusa amica se rompo
con queste parole sporche di mondo
se ti strofino e ti rigo
il marmoreo pavimento
la tua pagina bianca
ma fa freddo
e il mio cuore ancora batte
felice   disperato
lirico ed epico

Sandro Sardella is a poet and painter from Varese, area of Northern Italy. He read his poems in the 2012 San Francisco International Poetry Festival, where his painting were simultaneously exhibited at The Emerald Tablet Gallery. Translated by Jack Hirschman his "Coloredpaperbits" was published in San Diego in 1996 and others poems in "Five fingers review " – 19 in Berkeley in 2001. Some poems and drawing was published in: "Revolutionary Poets Brigade", in "Heartfire" and in "Overthrowing Capitalism" Vol.3 – Vol. 4.

America Loves Guns
More Than Children

America loves its guns more than its children.
America hunts down its children in the streets,
mows them down in the schools, massacres them in the malls.

American loves its guns more than its children.
Keeps its gun with it at all times, at all costs.
Would rather wage war than feed or educate poor kids.

Would rather everyone be armed than everyone be smart.
America loves its guns more than its children.
America carries its gun in the store, in the bar, in the church,

anywhere you might be – make you feel safe?
America loves its guns more than its children.
America buries its children – doesn't tuck them in at night,

doesn't read them stories in bed. Instead,
America, lonely & stressed, sleeps with its gun under its pillow.
America dreams of its guns – & wakes up groggy, & all wet.

America sells guns to crazy people,
sells weapons of war to madmen militias,
sells guns out of the trunks of its cars.

America loves its guns on tv, in the movies, on the news.
America loves its shooting range, its gun shows, its American Sniper.
America is entertained by its guns.

America coarsens young minds with gun culture.
America's love of guns kills love of life.
America blows its own Dream to bits.

Michael Castro

America buys guns & cuts education funding.
America loansharks its college students, "takes them out" with debt –
gives tax breaks to masters of war.

America loves its guns more than its children.
America loves its guns while its infrastructure crumbles.
America loves its guns while its air & water thicken & sicken.

America protects gun owners, neglects the environment.
NRA America says guns don't kill.
30,000 American deaths by guns per year.

America is armed & dangerous.

America makes bigger & better guns – sends its children off to battle.
America is world's biggest arms merchant.
American guns are big business. Big Business Are US.

America loves its guns while its jobs flee overseas.
America is mowing down its children right & left
in the streets, in the schools, in the malls;

Mowing them down right here today,
mowing down their present, mowing down their future.
America loves its guns more than its children.

Michael Castro is a poet, translator, arts activist and educator. Castro is co–founder of the literary organization and magazine River Styx and hosted the Poetry Beat radio show for fifteen years. He has been named one of St. Louis's top fifty writers by the Missouri History Museum, has received the Guardian Angel of St. Louis Poetry Award from River Styx, and been named a Warrior Poet by Word in Motion, all for lifetime achievement. The *St. Louis Post Dispatch* has called him "a legend in St. Louis Poetry." In 2015 he was named the first Poet Laureate of St. Louis.

How to Tell When a Resurrection Is at Hand... or, Evidence of Things Not Seen

like common
well-mannered thugs
they thought that
dumping the shrouded
body into the deep
would prevent multitudes
from rising up after
seeing the slain
corpse displayed.
guess again.
jihadis worship allah
not body displays
invoking anger
and the dumping
of dead flesh and
blood into the sea
has turned the
ocean into a
shrine touching
every shore. and
infidels once again
are dumb mofos.

after the flag-waving
lynch crowds
after the gloating
press conferences
after the presidential
visits to the various
death squads
after the ideological
media whore's
deadline filings
the dying and
killing goes on
there are new
recruits to the
jihadis from the
families that lost
their loved ones
to the drones
more soldiers are
coming home
dead or as physical
mental and moral

basket cases
to be replaced by
another batch of
lamb chops made
from our country's
young hoosiers
and hoodies
and the moment
has yet to arrive
when real or imagined
fisherman find a
white shroud caught
in their nets.
on that day, beware!
the shroud has
turned up without
the body and
the last time this
happened an
empire
was brought down

Gary Hicks　131

DALLAS AND BATON ROUGE, SUMMER 2016

for all of the fallen, no questions asked ... for now

mental disorders

a permanent feature

of colonial warfare

these days of spilt blood

consigning terror to verse

barely describes it

time of clarity

malcolm's chickens home roosting

specter of fanon

like a boomerang

what went around came around

from now on heads up!

Gary Hicks, emigre from Boston and resident of Berkeley CA, is the author of *a pen is like a piece. you pick it up. you use it,* and [with Tontongi] *The Dream of Being. His work has appeared in the People's Tribune, Compages, Nature Society and Thought, Asheville Poetry Review, Spare Change Newspaper,* and *Political Affairs.* Gary Hicks has been anthologized in two publications of Boston's Liberation Poetry Collective [of which he remains a member], *Poets Against the Killing Fields,* and *Liberation Poetry.* He is a member of the Revolutionary Poets Brigade in the San Francisco Bay Area. His book, Itching for Combat was published by VAGABOND in 2012

Gary Hicks

GEOMETRY B

He looks at palm trees
that stand outside
from the aluminum-framed
third floor window

There's a tennis court too
and a baseball diamond
both well-maintained inside
the chain link perimeter

A city of green arbors
and beveled-roof houses
with pairs of windows
on faces staring vacantly

Within the classroom filled
by students in desks
some dive into breakfast
carted-in in red and blue vinyl boxes

Today it's prepackaged
coffee cake "kind of dry"
which he observes is
enhanced via plastic spork

twisted around to make
a central circular hole to pour

cartoned Driftwood milk into
momentarily creating a little lake

Immediately absorbed
the white level drops
precipitously fast – too
quick for cellphone photo

Over the moist meal
teenagers discuss yesterday's
shooting at a downtown middle
school also in first period

"The twelve year old girl
must have been mad
at her boyfriend, and
shot the other side

in the wrist. Guess
she won't be texting
anybody for awhile."
They laugh and throw away

the empty containers
as the bell rings all walk
to the noisy hallway to
continue the academic day

Don Kingfisher Campbell, MFA in Creative Writing from Antioch University Los Angeles, has been a coach and judge for Poetry Out Loud, a performing poet/teacher for Red Hen Press Youth Writing Workshops, Los Angeles Area Coordinator and Board Member of California Poets In The Schools, publisher of Spectrum and the San Gabriel Valley Poetry Quarterly, leader of the Emerging Urban Poets writing and Deep Critique workshops, organizer of the San Gabriel Valley Poetry Festival, and host of the Saturday Afternoon Poetry reading series in Pasadena, California. http://dkc1031.blogspot.com

Don Kingfisher Campbell

AWAKENED

I have been awakened
by the rat-tat-tat of gunfire.

Bullets flying in classrooms.
Bullets flying in churches.
Bullets flying in mosques, through the streets,
in the subways, on playgrounds,
at dance clubs, everywhere,
everywhere, is a hail of bullets and
the bursting of bombs.

People shot while driving.
People shot while running away.
People shot while holding still,
hands up, in backyards, in the
doorway, waiting at Walmart,
shooters in uniform relentlessly
hitting their targets.

There is no prayer to fix this.

It is up to us to wake up, to
rise up; it is up to us to
organize, to march, to vote and
use our fragile bodies as our only
sturdy shield. It is up to us to
take back the streets –
Whose streets?
Our streets! –

by any means necessary.

Elizabeth S. Wolf

135

WHY WE MARCH FOR OUR LIVES

"They tell us to run, Mama,
they say make yourself tiny small
and silent quiet and hide in the
cupboard. We are not allowed to
play in the cupboard, Mama, only
to hide from the bad man who is shooting."

I cannot bear to hear
these words in a child's
voice. I cannot bear to
see what he is seeing.

"If the bad man shoots
your very best friend, Mama,
if he does, then you do not
cry. You pretend you are
dead too and maybe the bad man
will go away."

Do not tell me my child
should be kinder to others.
Dylan Klebold went to prom,
with a limo full of friends,
a week before the massacre.
Stuffing flowers in the barrels of guns
will not slow the bullet
nor staunch the flow of blood.

"Mama, I don't want to die
at school. Can I stay home with you?
We can tell teacher my tummy hurts.
I threw up after we hided. Teacher
wasn't mad. I think maybe she cried."

As I am weeping now
silently. Like Emma.
Like Barack after Newtown.
Like the mother holding the sign:
'Talk to me about the 2nd amendment
after your child has bled out
on the classroom floor.'

Who are these bad men
coming for our children?
Killing their ex-girlfriends?
Their want-to-be girlfriends,
their mothers-in-law, stepchildren,
slaughtering good people
gathering to pray?

Who. Are. These. Men.
We must know
what war we are fighting
in order to win.

Elizabeth S. Wolf writes because stories are how we make sense of our world. Elizabeth's poems appear in anthologies (Persian Sugar in English Tea; Amherst Storybook Project; Mosaics: A Collection of Independent Women; The Best of Kindness: Origami Poems Project) and journals (Ibbetson Street; New Verse News; Scarlet Leaf Review; Peregrine Journal). Elizabeth's chapbook "What I Learned: Poems" (Finishing Line Press) came out in October 2017. Her chapbook "Did You Know?" is a 2018 Rattle Chapbook Prize winner, coming in Summer 2019. Elizabeth has been an activist for a wicked long time.

Elizabeth S. Wolf

CHANT FOR OUR CHILDREN

Folks drove kids to school today
they came home dead, on NBC.
Two bullets ripped the hearts
a third, the heads, shot from
NRA's guns.

CNN

On the screen,
car pools to blood pools,
slick sound-bites at eleven,
babies on gurney bridges to heaven.

ABC

Over tented shrouds soiled, caked and stiff,
mamas' wails lift, but make no sense,
drowned by ambulances'
careening indifference.

CSPAN

Videoed Activists of every gripe
like kneeled nuns' necks stiffened to God,
chant the right to bear arms shall not be
abridged, while the right to raise kids shall.

Rolland Vasin

TRIBUTE TO MOTOWN

There's a formula for Motown. First
you kidnap Africans from their villages,
sell them as slaves to Americans who beat,
rape, murder, exploit, maim, demean them
for about, oh say, four-hundred years.
You deny them their native culture,
their music, their dance, self-expression.
Then you turn them loose on their own
for about another hundred years, still
continuing the abuse as when slaves.
You systematically deny them rights
of citizenship, and kill God's Children
when they assert those rights. But God
don't let only that bad happen. He leads
Brothers and Sisters be percussion,
be jazz, be soul, be fly. When those souls
swing, and sway, and tap, and writhe,
something comes out of their mouths
in melodious blood, and that be Motown.

Rolland Vasin (aka Vachine), a third generation American writer, published in the anthologies *Wide Awake* and *Coiled Serpent*, among others. Features at local performance venues, and reads open-mics from Coast to Coast. The Laugh Factory's 1992 3rd Funniest CPA in LA. His day job includes auditing Children's charities.

Rolland Vasin

Ma Barker at the D.O.C. (Dept. of Corrections)

The last two times, you came out
To meet your "boys" in the prison
They wouldn't even let you in,
Despite the fact that you spent
Over a quarter-century organizing
Poetry readings for the inmates
And it was the last thing
That Alzheimer's hadn't taken from you.

The first time they turned you away
It was because you forgot your I.D.
While the second time you forgot
To take off your watch before you went
Into the trap and they barred you
For the night because of that transgression.

The only kindness, much less justice,
In the whole thing was that you were
Persistent and patient as always and
Didn't seem to remember what
Had happened and calmly proceeded
To continue to do everything possible
To get to see your boys again.

James Van Looy

LABYRINTH:

THE 14TH ANNUAL MEMORIAL FOR THOSE WHO DIED HOMELESS ON THE STREETS AND IN THE SHELTERS OF THE COMMONWEALTH OF MASSACHUSETTS (JUST AFTER THE INVASION OF IRAQ IN 2003)

Here we are again at the center of the Labyrinth
of old cow path Boston near the fountain on the Common
whose bright green Spring May grass
floats cardboard tombstones
and each one bears at least one name
and this year for the first time many have more than one name
and a cut flower
and flags that fly on little sticks for the veterans.

There are almost too many to count especially
as seen from the distant golden state house dome.
Tell the native people who built the fish weir they found
on the other end of the Common about home sweet home.
We are all homeless Americans.
Great changes happen when the sky cries.
Brother Blue is really a doctor indeed a great healer.
Every word becomes a poem.

Fifteen years ago I scribed the names of the dead
on white crosses with black paint with a square brush,
and with a handful of disgruntled shelter workers pounded them
as stakes of protest into this earth at the heart of the city.
Long ago they said the Labyrinth was the symbol of the city maze
with a half man-half beast Minotaur monster at its center waiting
to devour the innocent children of the countryside in great bite,
but the Native Americans always knew it was really the Earth Mother.

James Van Looy

Now we gather for the 14th Annual Service for Those Who Died w/o a Home
and even the microphone and podium go silent in the falling tears.
Fifteen years ago there were about 60 names I painted on those crosses.
Last year there were more than 180 names.

This year there are 229.
Perhaps, this city Labyrinth is an engine of death?
Who is the Minotaur monster?
Where's Mom?

James Van Looy has been a fixture in Boston's poetry
venues since the 1970s. He performed with the Mirage
Mime Theater from 1980 to 1987 during which time he
also taught classes offered by Mirage. From 1987 to
1988 he was a member of the Collective Mime. His
poetry has been anthologized in *Out of the Blue Writers
Unite*. He has run poetry workshops for Boston area
homeless people at Pine Street Inn and St. Francis
House since 1992 and regularly reads at Bay State Prison as part of their poetry
program. Currently, Van Looy leads the Labyrinth Creative Movement Workshop. He
is the writer of *It's All One Thing*, a poem column for *Oddball Magazine*.

WATER IS LIFE

#NODAPL

H.LAMPERT / JUSTSEEDS.ORG

142

Aqua – Water

Thirsty lips
scratch like .33s
sun worn, warped
devoured by light
blessed, unnourished.
I pull my hand out of the ocean,
gold shades pull across my skin, wrapped
in seaweed and a Doritos bag.
I smell my fingers; oils rise like steam engines
mixed with salt; I keep my hands from my eyes.
Fearing the *mezcla* of stinging eyelids
with gasoline residue.
Smog inhalants under the fluffy clouds,
engineered birds droning coos
dropping spyware into my hair.
Sea birds run away from tides
and come back to nab a meal
buried 'neath the foliage of plastic sand –
wich baggies, Sunkist wrappers,
ragged land.

I walk upshore, tuck into dry sand
where I stare into the brown void
that is the sea. Tarnished gem –
Aqua gone, a green illusion under the blue.
Sailboats chart the route
between dying stingrays
twinkling, tangled above waters,
and a mattress laying portside,
springs turned up, spearing a silver fish;
unjust poacher. Unnatural relic.
I rub sand into my legs,
watch the pebbles trickle through my hairs –
dry stream of conscious deception,
the undrinkable, inhabitable body
barren home of waste.
On the California coast,
my heels sticky with tar;
"It's normal," I am told.

Jessica M. Wilson Cárdenas is a Chicana Poet born in East Los Angeles, CA. She is a 3rd generation Beatnik by way of Jack Spicer through Paul Vangelisti; with her MFA in Poetry from Otis College of Art and Design and BA in Creative Writing and Art History from UC Riverside. She is the founder of the Los Angeles Poet Society, (a bridge to LA's literary network), an educator and an activist. She is celebrating a win for best spoken word album from the 2018 Independent Music Awards, with Violinist Jenni Asher. Their album is called *Freedom*. Jessica's latest collection *Serious Longing* is available from Swan World Press, Paris, France. www.jessicamwilson.com | www.lapoetsociety.org

Jessica M. Wilson Cárdenas

MEDUSAS

Te mueves en un mar perplejo. Tus ojos desechan antiguas claridades en las que un árbol era un árbol, y la ardiente sal, un motivo para ir por el mundo.

Como los restos de un barco, te dejas abrazar por el oleaje. Tienes piedad de ti, y de aquello que dejaste en la orilla.

Abiertas medusas te rodean. Es verdad que todo tiende sus redes hacia ti en este instante. Quieres volver porque tienes miedo, pero ya es imposible. El secreto debe ser devorado completamente. Vuelves, sin embargo, dentro de ti, reconoces como cierto el rojo impulso que te lanzó al mar.

Respiras más allá de ti, más allá de nosotros. Haces que la carrera sea más larga. Te sigo de cerca sin saber, sintiendo cómo los días se desintegran, cómo el error va ganando altura y se arroja indiferente al vacío.

La piedra que sostuvo tus pies por un momento se hizo polvo antes de que pudieras arrepentirte. Para entonces todo estuvo de acuerdo; la luz, la línea exacta de la noche.

Cada vez más dócil al remolino, cada vez más dueña de la libertad de perderte. ¿Qué harás para llamarte en medio del fragor si en el horizonte azul se pierden también las palabras?

Deja que la corriente diluya entre nosotros este tiempo sin orillas.

Olivia Lott's translations of Colombian poetry have appeared most recently in *Mantis*, *Río Grande Review*, *Spoon River Poetry Review*, *Tupelo Quarterly*, and *Waxwing*. Her book-length translation (with Barbara Jamison), *The Dirty Text* by Cuban poet Soleida Ríos, is forthcoming with Kenning Editions. Olivia is currently a Ph.D. student and Olin Fellow in Hispanic Studies and Translation Studies at Washington University in St. Louis.

Lucía Estrada

Medusa Jellyfish

You move about in a baffled sea. Your eyes cast aside ancient clarities from when a tree was a tree, and the red-hot sand, a reason to go through life.

Like scraps of a boat, you let the swell embrace you. You take pity on yourself, on what you left behind on the shore.

Open jellyfish surround you. Right now it's true that everything dangles their nets towards you. You want to go back because you're scared, but it's no longer possible. The secret should be swallowed whole. Still, you're back, inside yourself, aware of the reality of the red impulse that threw you to the sea.

You're breathing beyond yourself, beyond us. You make the road longer. I follow you closely without you noticing, feeling how the days come apart, how error picks up altitude and plunges, detached, into nothingness.

The stone that shouldered your feet for a moment turned to dust before you had a chance to say you're sorry. By then everything was just right; the light, night's precise line.

More and more powerless to the whirlpool, more and more in control of the freedom of losing you. How will you call for yourself in the middle of the uproar if words, too, get lost in the blue horizon?

Let the current dilute this shoreless time between us.

Translated from the Spanish by Olivia Lott

Lucía Estrada (Medellín, Colombia, 1980) is the prize-winning author of 10 books of poetry, including *Las Hijas del Espino* (2006), *El Ojo de Circe* (2007), *La noche en el espejo* (2010), and *Cuaderno del ángel*(2012). She recently won the Bogotá Poetry Prize for her forthcoming collection *Katábasis.* She has been invited to participate in many national and international literary events and, for several years, she was one of the directors of the groundbreaking Medellín International Poetry Festival. Her work has been partially translated into English, French, Japanese, Italian and German.

Lucía Estrada

HOOKED

You cannot lure wonder
no matter how you yearn
for trees and sky. Nature
will tease us with her light.

Once we are hooked on that
glimpse of dangling moon,
we're confined to the jail
of the concrete city.

Judged for our careless desires,
we float in shadowy
rooms, croon old promises,
bleed money like clouds.

If roofs were made of air
our spirits could go free.
If balloons were birds, we
would know our destiny.

If flags were rivers, we'd
be faithful to the sun.
Everything we see
mirrors our spreading want.

Once we left our nature,
left the song of our home.
Babies escape their pools,
then hunger for water.

Terry Wolverton is the author of eleven books of poetry, fiction and creative nonfiction, including *Embers*, a novel in poems, and *Insurgent Muse: life and art at the Woman's Building*, a memoir. Her most recent title is *RUIN PORN*, a collection of poems. She is the founder of Writers At Work, a creative writing studio in Los Angeles, and Affiliate Faculty in the MFA Writing Program of Antioch University Los Angeles. http://terrywolverton.com

Terry Wolverton

I...Am

I am the kid who grew up 4th Ave and Exposition Place.
The kid who went to Dublin elementary from third to 5th grade before the name was changed to Tom Bradley.
I'm the kid who lived on 49th and Normandie.
The kid who caught the yellow school bus to Audubon Middle school playing with Pokémon cards before moving to Palmyra Road, which was much closer.
I am the kid who survived childhood with a single mother of 5 watching Doug, Power Rangers, Recess, and Yugi-Oh eating Cinnamon Toast Crunch as my Saturday morning routine where hearing about someone's death was normal at the table.

I am the teen who grew up in what people call 'The Jungles'
The teen who graduated from Dorsey High School despite the violence, gang activity, and stereotypes associated around me.
I am the teen who lived in the University dorms at Cal State LA;
The young adult preparing to graduate, obtaining his Bachelor's degree in Social Work
I am Truth
I am lies
I am mistakes
I am corrections
I am the person frowning when a cigarette has been sparked.
That driver who has somewhere to be
EVERY time I get in the car and honks at people for text driving.
Some call it road rage,
I call it using the car for what it's for.
I am the creative adult that survived,
So when people with the slightest clue ask
"Who are you?" I simply reply
I am human,
Just like you.

Rondell E. Johnson

147

THE GHETTO

We from the Ghetto
Where they thought we would be helpless
Thought we would want nothing more than sex, drugs and alcohol
Built jails setting shit up for us to spend our days in a cell
But little did they know
We would grind in the Ghetto
Shine in the Ghetto
G-H-E-T-T-O
We Grinding Hard Even Through the Obstacles
The story isn't over though,
Some rather hear words along the lines of
Money, Cars, Clothes, and Hoes
Promoting anything and everything that has nothing to do with accomplishing Real Goals
While the Devil is out here snatching up all Souls as collateral, in exchange for a stack of
faces that we like to call dough.
From the Ghetto
From the North, South,
East to the West,
We all got a Ghetto.
Functioning with the 5 P's in mind,
Properly preparing myself to Prevent Poor Performance
Every day from the challenges we face right here,
In the Ghetto.

Rondell E. Johnson (RJ The Poet) is a Writer and Multimedia artist from
Los Angeles, California. RJ is active in his community doing volunteer work
with a Small Press, Campaigning a Premier weekly event in Hollywood, and
training to soon be working as an Emergency Medical Technician. The Los
Angeles native aims to encourage, inspire, and uplift people from all walks
of life, especially Black & Brown youth, sharing personal experiences
through creative expression.

Rondell E. Johnson

IT'S A JUNGLE OUT THERE

Motorhomes park clinically by the beach;
These are not psychedelic Dormobiles
Or battered vans with mattresses
Spread out on old carpets,
These are sprayed battleship grey
And their occupants hide
Behind tinted windows,
They have special fixings
For bikes and equipment,
Not just faded surf boards
Lashed to rusty roof racks.

Someone in the pier bar
Told me that at night,
When the coast is clear,
Shadowy figures emerge
And empty chemical toilets
Onto the seashore;
I said I didn't believe that,
Which was received
With mocking laughter
And a shake of the head,
Surely such things don't happen.

Surely within those sleek
Expensive vehicles
The technology exists
For proper waste disposal,
Surely such bad behaviour
Doesn't happen and anyway
Shouldn't we welcome tourists,
Instead of spreading negativity;
My drinking friend disagreed
Whispering drunkenly in my ear
'It's a jungle out there'.

David Subacchi

149

BUILDING A PRISON

They're building a prison
with many construction jobs
and more when operational.
The governor is appointed.
His face well known.

No industrialist wanted the site
but it's served by public roads.
A win-win situation some say.
Other people are worried.
They don't matter.

Modern engineering allows
the roof to be bolted on
before the walls are added.
Those old walls that ensure
it is a place of confinement.

David Subacchi lives in Wales (UK) where he was born of Italian
roots. He studied at the University of Liverpool. He has four
published collections of his English Language poetry and one in
Welsh.

150 **David Subacchi**

CHI AVRÀ IL CORAGGIO DI GUARDARE NEGLI OCC HI LE FUTURE GENERAZIONI?

L'isola di plastica del Pacifico
s'ingrandisce a macchia d'olio,
pescherecci pescano a strascico
diffondendo anche la nostra
morte nei mari che potrebbero
smettere di produrre
ossigeno, chi pagherà
per questo? no, non noi,
ma quelli che verranno ai quali
lasceremo inquinamento
e ignoranza e una lotta
per la sopravvivenza
senza precedenti.
Oppure
da oggi dobbiamo dare vita
al Rinascimento ecologico
fotovoltaico elettrico:
mai più petrolio in Brasile!
Quando ero un ragazzo
questa era fantascienza,
ora è a portata di mano
purché i popoli lo vogliano,
dobbiamo dissuadere la Cina
dall'utilizzo del carbone
e quando lo stile di vita

sarà occidentale
e consumistico in India
deve essere eco sostenibile
per non ripetere il nostro
scempio.
Autonomia energetica
ecologica in Russia
e Sud Africa
così da diffondere benessere
ovunque, che farà deporre
le armi e creerà occupazione,
educazione, una nuova era
di democrazia planetaria
dove governi l'Onu e ogni
semestre cambi il Paese guida
in modo da dar voce anche
al resto del mondo.
Questo è un sogno
ma non è utopia
e sono sicuro la specie
umana sia pronta ad evolversi
per tornare a rispettare
la nostra grande, ma fragile
madre terra.

152

Igor Costanzo

WHO'LL HAVE THE COURAGE TO LOOK THE FUTURE GENERATION IN THE EYES?

The island of plastic in Pacific
increasing in oil spills;
fishing boats drag-fish
and spreading our
death in seas that could
stop producing
oxygen. Who will pay
for this? No, not us
but those will come to whom
we'll leave pollution
and ignorance and a struggle
to survive that'll be
without precedence.
Or else
from today on we have to give birth
to the electric photovoltaic
ecological Renaissance:
never again oil in Brazil!
When I was a boy
this was science fiction;
now it's within reach:
we have to dissuade China
from utilizing carbon,
and when lifestyle
in India becomes western
and consumeristic
it's got to be eco-sustainable
so as not to repeat the western
havoc.
Energetic ecological
autonomy in Russia
and South Africa
so that by spreading well-being
everywhere, it will disarm
weaponry and create jobs,
education, a new era
of planetary democracy
where the U.N. governs and
every six months the leading country changes
by way of giving voice as well
to the rest of the world.
This is a dream
but it's not utopia
and I'm sure mankind's
ready to evolve
through returning to respect
our grand but fragile
mother earth.

Igor Costanzo Poet, writer and performer. His books: *I Wish to Be Light* (C.C.Marimbo, 2005) edited and translated by Jack Hirschman. *Innocenza in bilico* (Zanetto editore, 2007) with an afterword by Alda Merini. In 2010 he founded the Volo Press Edizioni, having published books by Paul Polansky, Enrico Ghedi, Beppe Costa. He is also the co-founder and curator of the Moniga Art Festival, Italy's first environmental festival.

Igor Costanzo

WORK ETHIC

Unemployed,
if working age.
Unused.
No paid work,
so, nothing earned.
Meagre cash,
only that doled
by a reluctant state.
No use.
No value.
No respect
where cash is king
and work is queen,
no job,
no use,
no point,
no purpose.
No means
of change.

Lynn White

I Saw a Bird

I saw a bird today,
just one.
I wasn't alone,
many people saw it,
more came out to look
dusting off their long unused
binoculars.
Facebook was buzzing
like the insects used to buzz.
And so many tweets
trending for all those lost tweeters.
It made the local headlines,
then the national ones.
It flew a long way that bird,
then it was gone.

Lynn White lives in north Wales. Her work is influenced by issues of social justice and events, places and people she has known or imagined. She is especially interested in exploring the boundaries of dream, fantasy and reality. Her poem 'A Rose For Gaza' was shortlisted for the Theatre Cloud 'War Poetry for Today' competition 2014. This and many other poems, have been widely published in anthologies and journals such as Apogee, Firewords, Pilcrow & Dagger, Indie Soleil, Light and Snapdragon.

foto Marco Cinque

156

HAITI, LAND OF THE MOUNTAINS

Haiti, land of the mountains
Haiti, land of the Taino
Land of restorative justice
Land of suffering
Land of rape and pillage
Gifts of the Spanish, the French, the Americans
A land whose stories do not end in justice or peace or moral lessons
A land whose stories end in blood
A land who remembers the Taino maiden from Boriken
Who washed her father's rainbow belt by the river
When a Spaniard on a horse saw her beauty
Killed her father with his huge white dog
Raped her brutally
And cut off her head
So her body would be unrecognized
The Taino lived peaceably
In the Caribbean
Always peaceably
Among enemies
Who enslaved them
Enslaved them to work the plantations
Until one day
In Haiti,
An enslaved people
Repudiated their slavery
And won their independence
Only to be punished again

Karen Melander-Magoon

157

Indentured by the powerful colonialists
Made to pay blood money for their bodies and labor
Oh unhappy imperialists with slaves
Worried that a free Haiti
Would corrupt other slave economies
With the wish for freedom
Oh let us cut off the head of Haiti
So the ownership of its beauty may not be recognized
Its people unrecognized, anonymous
Punish its arrogance
The arrogance of a savage, invisible island people
Rape its soul, rape its land, its forests
Pollute its waters
Rain horror on its people in the city and land of the sun
Till there is nothing left but disease and poverty
In a gentle people's
Paradise

ROQUE DALTON, MARTYR IN 1975

(San Salvador, El Salvador, 14 May 1935 – Quezaltepeque, El Salvador, 10 May 1975)

He was killed by his brothers, his friends, his fellow rebels
He wrote of the poor who lived on anything and nothing
Of death in love rather than death in hate
Those who feared the poet threatened him
With the slander of betrayal
Threatened to smear his red ghost
The ghost that died betrayed
O Roque, you knew the sounds of nature
Crickets and growing things
In fields of El Salvador
You knew the sounds of crying babies
Encircled by massacring armies
Hiding in those same fields
Starved as their mothers died
Killed as they screamed
You knew the sounds of hate
And the sounds of love
You knew Cuba
You knew Prague
You knew Diego Rivera
You knew revolution
And you were a poet
A soldier of truth
Killed
For your belief
In life
And justice

Karen Melander–Magoon, D.Min., holds a Bachelors Degree in Music from Indiana University, sang major roles in opera for nearly two decades in Europe and has composed four one–woman musical portraits of historical figures, including Clara Barton, Georgia O'Keeffe, Lillie Langtry, and the French poet, Colette. She is listed in the European Publishers VIP Who is Who. Karen has a Masters in Counseling from Boston University, as well as her Doctor of Ministry from San Francisco Theological Seminary.

Karen Melander-Magoon

A BOLIVIAN BEATITUDE✤

And when Bechtel, the neoliberal conquistador
murmured, "I thirst for a greater return on my investments,"
Bolivia's governor and legislators did hear his cry
and filled with compassion for their boss's bottom line,
privatized Cochabamba's municipal water supply

But when the indigenous compesinos of Cochabamba
like the companero carpenter on Golgotha cross cried,
"WE THIRST," they were told they first
had to pay their water bill

They then asked how were they going to be able to pay
as much as one quarter of their two dollars a day income
and still get by

Government and corporation spokesmen explained sacrifices
must be made for the structural adjustment which would insure
a more efficient market but if they were patient, wealth from
Bechtel investment would trickle down to them by and by

But when the rains came, the people of Cochabamba
discovered Bechtel had claimed even the water
which fell from the sky and they were prohibited
from gathering rainwater

"The water didn't come from that pendejo so why
in hell is he charging us for it," they asked?
But when the people saw how their government defended
the private property rights of a corporation over their sacred
right to drink water, they took to the streets shouting,
"THE WATER IS OURS, DAMN IT!"

They sent the police
They shot tear gas
Two children blinded
The companeros marched on shouting,

Carl "CaLokie" Stilwell

**"EL PUEBLO UNIDO
JAMAS SERA VENCIDO"**

They sent the army
They fired guns
Six killed and 175 wounded
The companeros marched on shouting,
**"EL PUEBLO UNIDO
JAMAS SERA VENCIDO"**

At the climax of the struggle –
The police remained in their stations
The army stayed in their barracks
The members of Congress became invisible
The Governor went into hiding and afterwards resigned
The only legitimate authority left was
**"EL PUEBLO UNIDO
JAMAS SERA VENCIDO"**

The people gathered at the city square
making decisions in large assemblies
And at the end they made
the decisions about the water

Blessed are those whose thirst for justice
will never be quenched until it rolls down like
mighty waters from an ever flowing stream

*⁺This poem is based on an interview with Oscar Olivera,
Coalition of Water and Life, from the documentary, Corporation.*

Carl "CaLokie" Stilwell I was born during the depression in Oklahoma
and came to Pasadena, in 1959 to go to Fuller Theological Seminary.
But instead of becoming a preacher I became a teacher and taught in
the Los Angeles Unified School District for over 30 years. I have poems
published in the Altadena Poetry Review, Blue Collar Review, Canary,
Intersections, Lummox, Pearl, The Rise Up Review, Spectrum and
Struggle. My pen name was inspired by the Joads struggle for survival
in *The Grapes of Wrath* and the songs and life of Woody Guthrie.

HA LA MIA GENTE?

che cosa
la mia gente
ha?
ha
la mia gente
rabbia, pregiudizi
scheletri nell'armadio
odii, nemici
disagi mentali
rancori
disturbi della crescita
aggressività, bugie
illusioni in cui
nascondersi
ha
la mia gente
paura

che cosa
la mia gente
ha?
ha
la mia gente
polizia, istituzioni
porte blindate
dittature
corruzione
sopraffazione
politici
troppo simili

a sé
povertà
che non si sa
colmare
vizi, pigrizia
demoni
da soddisfare
ha
la mia gente
paura

che cosa
la mia gente
ha?
ha
la mia gente
tecnologia
vestiti alla moda
hi-tech all'ultimo
grido
amici virtuali
nemici reali
suonerie, gadget
bolidi che arrivano
inutilmente
ai 200
notizie incontrollate
informazione manipolata
e-banking troppo facile
portafogli vuoti

orologi per calcolare
tempo non suo
carta stampata
e già straccia
ha
la mia gente
paura

che cosa
la mia gente
ha?
ha
la mia gente
diritti fasulli
ospedali sforniti
scuole cadenti
debiti, tasse
strade dissestate
istituti privati
che privano
banche, franchising
brand, vetrine
sport in TV
giustizia falsata
rotatorie, bancomat
cosmesi
musica scaricata
artisti per strada
la verità in mano
la verità in vendita

Matteo Rimi   163

inquinamento
e nessuna volontà
di smettere
ha
la mia gente
paura

che cosa
la mia gente
ha?
ha
la mia gente
parenti, passato
memoria selettiva
occhi foderati
sentimenti stagni
indifferenza
su ciò
che non ingrassa
o arricchisce
sensibilità retrattili
sostanze che
annebbiano
oscurano
azzerano
schiavizzano
annientano

ha
la mia gente
paura

che cosa
la mia gente
ha?
ha
la mia gente
pulsioni
corpi da soddisfare
protesi, ritocchi
gesti inconsulti
atti sconsiderati
chili in eccesso
chili in difetto
personal trainer
abusi di calorie
voglia di correre
come fuggire
OGM, fast food
ormoni
a casaccio
attrezzi non atti
a sollevare dubbi
creme emollienti
emollient

rilassanti
ringiovanenti
creme
pasticciere
per addolcire
il vero
bilance
da tenere
come altari
ha
la mia gente
paura

che cosa
la mia gente
ha?
ha
la mia gente
una luce
profonda
capace
di effondere
in là
di questo
ha
la mia gente
paura

WHAT HAVE MY PEOPLE?

What
have
my people?
My people
have
anger, prejudices
skeletons in the closet
hates, enemies
mental discomforts
grudges
growth disorders
aggressiveness, lies
illusions in which
hide themselves
my people
have
fear

What
have
my people?
My people
have
police, institutions
armored doors
dictatorships
corruption
oppression
too much
like them
politicians
poverty
that we can not
fill up
vices, laziness

demons
to satisfy
my people
have
fear

What
have
my people?
My people
have
technology
fashionable clothes
state-of-the-art
hi-tech
virtual friends
real enemies
ringtones, gadgets
cars arriving
uselessly
at 200
uncontrolled news
manipulated information
too easy e-banking
empty wallets
clocks measuring
not their time
stamped and already
ruined
paper
my people
have
fear

What

have
my people?
My people
have
fake rights
unequipped hospitals
falling schools
debts, taxes
rough roads
privating private
institutes
banks, franchising
brands, showcases
sport in TV
false justice
roundabouts, cash
machines
cosmetics
downloaded music
musicians out on the
street
truth in your hand
truth on sale
pollution
and no will
to stop
my people
have
fear

What
have
my people?
My people
have

Matteo Rimi   165

relatives, past
selective memory
bacon-wrapped bug eyes
waterproof feelings
indifference
to this
that isn't fattening
or enriching
retractile sensitivities
substances that
cloud
obscure

reset
enslave
annihilate
my people
have
fear

What
have
my people?
My people

have
instincts
bodies to satisfy
prosthesis, touch-ups
rush gestures
rash acts
excessive kilos
missing kilos
personal trainers
calorie abuses
will to run
like escape
OGM, fast foods
hormones
at random
tools not apt
to raise doubts

o
relaxing
rejuvenating creams
pastry
creams
to sweeten

the truth
libras
to hold
like altars
my people
have
fear

What
have
my people?
My people
have
a deep
light
able
to effuse
right there
of this
my people
have
fear

Matteo Rimi was born in Castelfiorentino and lives in Fiesole, Florence (Italy), where he is a councilor of the Associazione Artisti Fiesolani. Graduated in Foreign Languages and Literatures, he then started working in healthcare. Lover of the Beat Generation, for his thesis he made an interesting interview to Lawrence Ferlinghetti in Genoa in 2002 during the Poetic Revolution that involved writers such as Antonio Bertoli and Alejandro Jodorowsky. He has edited a column for the e-magazine Cultura Commestibile, "The State of Poetry", making interviews with the most important Florentine poets and thus making friends and collaborations. He is a member of 100 Thousand Poets for Change Movement, organizing events and translating during the 100TPC World Conference in 2015 in Salerno, Italy.

PORTRAIT OF A HOMELESS YOUTH WITH LIZARD

Gabriel woke
up near the Hollywood
Freeway, sleeping
on his side, under
a brush and smog. As the sun
rose from the East, he noticed
a creature nestled between
the earth and his belly.

Gabriel slowly moved
his hand offering it
to the creature. It wrapped
around Gabriel's hand, making
him smile.

Gabriel
named the lizard, Hope, placing
it on his shoulder. Wherever
Gabriel went, Hope went. Whenever
Gabriel ate, Hope ate. Whenever
Gabriel slept, Hope slept.

When people asked where
he found his lizard, Gabriel
liked to say, "I didn't find
Hope; Hope found
me."

Nikolai Garcia grew up in South Central Los Angeles; currently works with homeless youth in the East Hollywood area; and has been sleeping in Compton for the last 15 years. He has been published in Huizache, Dryland, Statement and a few other literary journals. If poetry readings had walk-up music, (like at baseball games), his song of choice would be between YG's "Twist My Fingaz," and Celso Piña's "Cumbia Sobre el Rio." He sometimes makes friends on social media: @HelloKommie

Nikolai Garcia

DO YOU BELIEVE IN FORGIVENESS?

You say you do, Then why use tools of absolution.
Hated when we bear arms. hated when we remove them. No methods proven.
I hate neither the tool, nor tailor, not the craft, nor creator,
Such that, Regardless of color, I see that we are all slaves.
Slaves to the shadows that bear witness to every silent scream,
every missing persons, or mass murder.
Slaves to Shadows that witness every one of my wounds
while being shot in my back as I ran further.
Slaves enraged. Because instead of a warning when my neighbor, friends, or my own
actions intended to injure loved ones, there was a darkened silhouette
where the mouth of a man should've been.
Slaves unable to speak because they are so simply manufactured,
they were never given the sight, mind, or heart to be human.
Their indistinguishableness stands affixed behind us all.
A place where our darkest selves lie,
Our absolution, for retribution, will be life's conclusion.
Unable to speak life because the very thing that we arm ourselves with does not live.
It's fed bullets to breath, cyclic fire in its sneeze,
a monster of greed who takes without the ability to give?
A hammer can tear down while simultaneously building from the destruction,
You shoot me. You will never be able to put those broken pieces
of either our lives back together.
That destruction is what you're stuck in.
Wars are won with guns, while cowards hide behind the shields of men,
My voice is cracked, but I still speak because it's a place I frequent,
a state of mind where I have been,
Time and time again, I have pulled men's souls
out of the unforgiving grasp of death from your weapons,
Your absolution, for retribution, will be life's conclusion,
It is my job to survive with Men who will never be the same. So have we really?
I have held innocent children in my arms comfortable, until they've wished to breathe no
more, Walked on roads stained the color of sadness.

168 **Devin Smith**

So what happened?
Our eyes were fixed on an equal future,
Souls standing in solidarity, screaming secrets and sharing stories,
Love with the only condition being that we were able to love.
My ancestors would unravel like raw wool in the wind at the work that is being undone,
We are unable to remember who we are,
The hate was not a secret and now the love is a lie,
Black on black violence is as oxymoronic as white on white,
You kill who you are closest to. Like a lover who callously breaks heart with severed ties.
We don't know how to love anymore and that's ok,
We think these plastic people, those paper properties can fill the voids within ourselves,
Some voids are too great, depression so abysmal they fill themselves with these shells,
See how your absolution, for retribution, will be loves conclusion,
Capitulated addenda's from professional liars whom would swiftly sale the value of their children's souls for a seat in a house where no one represented.
Remember this!
The antagonist creates his important purpose in life.
Death by the hands of man is beyond the contemplation of wrong or right.
It does this thing to the spirit, but makes sure the flesh is fine.
Lastly if it can be done... with a gun... it can be done... with a knife!
Hate without reason is the deadliest of diseases.
A Poison... with only one cure....
You!

Devin Smith attended College for psychology and is currently finishing his bachelors. He's a 26 year old Active duty Combat Veteran with the United States Army and now oversees Medical Logistics, medical training, and The Army Suicide Prevention program for the Warrior Center where some of the most elite Army National Guard and Active Duty Soldiers across all branches are trained. Smith's goal is to gain the financial capital to remove generational poverty from his family tradition. Smith owns guns, but believes that it is the character of a man that will stand the test of time. Character! If only we could do a background check for that! Smith's story has recurring motifs throughout this snapshot of his history. 1. Though at times of extreme loneliness, we are not and will not be alone. 2. Everything is connected, and there will be someone on your journey who will help you into the next stage of your life. 3. To be a man, you must see men. Or universally applied, "To be a success, you must witness success".

foto Marco Cinque

170

THE AMERICAN ANTHEM

It's you, America.
Murdered your best children
Not the terrorist from outside.

You, who unjustly executed
Those who could change
Those who could realize
Your Dream, those who could
Stop the nightmare you woke us up in.

It's you, America, that you killed.
In cold blood
Martin Luther King, Malcolm X
Robert Kennedy, Harvey Milk
After killing and divested
The children of Sitting Bull and enslaved
An entire people kidnapped in Africa.

It's you, America, that you're in and you're in
Killing, raving about progress
Of freedom smothered in your gas chambers
Roasted on your electric chairs
Locked in your cities-prison
Put on your filthy fast food.

Look in the uncomfortable mirror of truth:
You'll find it's you, America, that you use your
Same Constitution to wipe your gross ass
Of Profits, you declaring "Humanitarian Wars"
To sell us your weapons to use after having them
Aim at our temples, you thinning to the ground
Beauty in every conjugation
To Oil the bloody gears that
They move the reconstruction business.

Marco Cinque   171

It is you, America, who finance terror.
That you grow your grandchildren Nazi, your
Ku-Klux-Klan, Your Coups, your dictators
With your seven of fanatics and racists, your
Services and counter-intelligence, FBI the CIA
Your Atomic Massacres, your napalm.
Your depleted uranium, your white phosphorus
The killing is torture: Abu Ghraib & Guantanamo.

It's you, America, that you believe Samson
You, that if it collapses, the world collapses.
You who hate and despise but want to be loved
With your veins of oil and global rating
With your markets that soil billions of lives
In your streets crowded by poor and defeated
You puking nationalism at saddles & stripes
You Megalomaniac Sheriff of the apocalypse.

It's you, America, that disown your wrinkles
You with your fake lips, your silicone
Your corrupt body to the root
Your Oscar Awards, the ridiculous Nobel quotes
Your Olympic propaganda medals.

Sing again if you can, sing with your hand
On the heart, that when you find out you don't have one
And you will recognize in that feral heartbeat a chime
Funeral that always soul you and moves you, then
Your tattered flag of lies flies
On the painted tomb of your democracy.

Maybe you'll cry a shame you never had.
Look at the eye for an eye that blinds you.
The Pentagon and the empire, you will stop the embargo on Cubans.
Finally recognizing a new American Dream:
Mother Earth, along with the last of the Mohicans.

CONTROCANTO ALL'INNO AMERICANO

Sei tu, America, tu che hai
assassinato i tuoi figli migliori
non il terrorista venuto da fuori.

Tu, che hai ingiustamente giustiziato
coloro che potevano cambiarti
coloro che potevano realizzare
il tuo sogno, coloro che potevano
impedire l'incubo in cui ci hai svegliati.

Sei tu, America, che hai ammazzato
a sangue freddo premeditato
Martin Luther King, Malcom X
Robert Kennedy, Harvey Milk
dopo aver sterminato e spossessato
i figli di Sitting Bull e schiavizzato
un intero popolo rapito all'Africa.

Sei tu, America, che ti stai e ci stai
uccidendo, vaneggiando di progresso
di libertà soffocata nelle tue camere a gas
arrostita sulle tue sedie elettriche
rinchiusa nelle tue città-prigione
ingrassata dai tuoi luridi fast-food.

Guardati nello specchio scomodo della verità:
scoprirai che sei tu, America, che usi la tua
stessa Costituzione per pulirti quel culo lordo
di profitti, tu che dichiari "guerre umanitarie"
per venderci le tue armi da usare, dopo averle
puntate alle nostre tempie, tu che radi al suolo
la bellezza in ogni sua coniugazione
per oliare gli ingranaggi maledetti che
muovono il business della ricostruzione.

Sei tu, America, che finanzi il terrore
che cresci i tuoi nipoti nazifascisti, il tuo
Ku-Klux-Klan, i tuoi golpe, i tuoi dittatori
con le tue Sette di fanatici e razzisti, i tuoi
servizi e contro-servizi segreti, l'FBI la CIA
i tuoi massacri atomici, il tuo napalm
il tuo uranio impoverito, il tuo fosforo bianco
le tue torture: Abu Ghraib & Guantanamo.

Marco Cinque 173

Sei tu, America, che ti credi Sansone
tu, che se crolli crollasse pure il mondo
tu che odi e disprezzi ma che vuoi essere amata
con le tue vene pulsanti di petrolio e rating globale
coi tuoi mercati che radono al suolo miliardi di vite
nelle tue strade affollate da poveri e sconfitti
tu che vomiti nazionalismo a selle & strisce
tu, megalomane sceriffo dell'apocalisse.

Sei tu, America, che disconosci le tue rughe
tu con le tue labbra rifatte, il tuo silicone
il tuo corpo corrotto fino alla radice
i tuoi premi Oscar, i ridicoli Nobel preventivi
le tue medaglie olimpiche di propaganda.

Canta ancora se ci riesci, canta con la mano
sul cuore, che quando scoprirai di non averne uno
e riconoscerai in quel ferale battito un rintocco
funebre che da sempre ti anima e ti muove, allora
la tua bandiera stracciata di bugie sventolerà
sul sepolcro imbiancato della tua democrazia.

Forse piangerai una vergogna che non hai mai avuto
ripudierai l'occhio per occhio che t'acceca, abolirai
il Pentagono e l'Impero, smetterai l'embargo ai cubani
riconoscendo finalmente un nuovo sogno americano:
la Madre Terra, assieme all'ultimo dei Moicani.

Marco Cinque was born in Rome in 1957. In 1992 he began an correspondence with two Native Americans on the death row of San Quentin. Several times he visited San Quentin to promote numerous projects, including the national campaign Adopting a convicted: epistolary adoptions of prisoners held on US death row. He also carried out numerous projects in many Italian prisons, both with writing and music laboratories and taking care of the publication of many works carried out by inmates and inmates. He writes, photographs, plays, recites, publishes essays, poetic collections, articles. Participates in music albums, international poetry festivals, pictorial and photographic exhibitions. He's published more than 30 books and has been translated into Spanish, French and English.

IMMIGRANT

Time, the ever-present observer of all things!
We live it.
We see it pass.
We are aware of it weaving its way through generations,
taking notes of the developing stories.
The tale of the immigrant:
past,
present,
future.
If time could talk, it would spin the fascinating tale of the immigrant;
living, breathing beings with a beautiful story entwined in history.
They were called many things:
explorers, wanderers, traders, fortune hunters,
persecuted, persecutors, conquerors, usurpers,
seekers of knowledge, seekers of religious freedom,
heroes, saviors, plunderers, murderers.
An ancient story of the far away;
immigrants who fought great odds,
who sailed great distances into the unknown.
Time would tell us the story
of the Pilgrims, of Ponce de León and his quest for the fountain of youth,
of Christopher Columbus and the so-called discovery of the Americas
with his desire to take the riches of the established pre-Hispanic civilizations.
A story of the immigrant life of restlessness,
A story of a kingdom
forged by those early immigrants.
Time would also tell the compelling story of today's immigrants:
the immigrants sometimes hidden under luggage,
hidden with their hopes and dreams
from the prying, probing eyes of law-enforcement officers.
They are called by many names;
migrants, naturalized citizens, newcomers, incomers,
documented, undocumented, aliens, illegal aliens,
day crossers, dreamers.
Time watches them as they continue to come:

Arcea Zapata de Aston

175

yesterday,
today,
tomorrow.
They come with their dreams,
their hopes, their desires,
their fears.
Time watches them as they continue to come and plant new seeds,
seeds that take root
in California, in Arizona,
in Michigan, in Illinois, in New York,
take root in the south and north,
east and west,
in every part of a nation that can be
welcoming, open-armed,
begrudging or hateful.
Immigrants, different in many ways from those early immigrants,
coming without the desire to conquer nor escaping from harmful arms
but rather of simply bringing their belongings,
their hopes,
their dreams.
Dreams of raising children,
dreams of passing a better life to them.
Time simply smiles and says,
"Let me introduce you to my fraternal twin, Change."
You can either fight Change
or embrace Change.
But, Time and Change will always be with us.

 Professor **Arcea Zapata de Aston** has a bachelor's degree in philology and languages (Universidad del Atlántico, Colombia) and a Master's degree in the Spanish language and Spanish American literature (University of Arkansas in Fayetteville). She holds a doctoral degree in Latin American literature with emphasis in poetry (University of Iowa). She has extensive teaching experience both domestically and abroad at several universities in Colombia and in the United States. She is editing and revising materials to complete a book on female subjectivity in the postmodernist poetry of Delmira Agustini, Juana de Ibarbourou, and Alfonsina Storni. She is also putting together a manuscript on women as hostages of societal discourse using the imaginary of the body in the *libro de buen amor*, *La Celestina*, and *La lozana andaluza*.

A Convergence at the Border

Marching side by side,
two by two
staying on the sidewalk,
as the legal observers advised.
Chanting something that feels determined,
it didn't matter the language of the words,
it was the rhythm that made them one undulating dragon
marching to the border
in the hot desert sun.

But I am Mariposa de la Gente Amable.
I fly by my own laws
I freely cross your cruel walls
however high.
I just flutter my wings and fly!

I flew among them in the hot sun,
uplifted by their spirited chant.
Some noticed me and smiled.
Some were too preoccupied
to see anything as free as me.
Such sad creatures,
forced by the laws of physics and biology
to remain rooted to the earth;
forced by the laws of politics and greed
to be separated by papers and steel.

Possession of documents let some cross,
to a place with the same houses, same shops, same gentle people,
knowing they could return.
Without papers,
just one step into that other country

Jeeni Criscenzo

and you will be forever separated.
Kind, hard working or brilliant...
all that matters is that damned document.

But I am Mariposa de la Gente Amable.
I fly by my own laws
I freely cross your cruel walls
however high.
I just flutter my wings and fly!

I flew gaily among them
as hundreds arrived,
on both sides of that slithering serpent of rusted steel
as if they had restrained your magnificent Quetzalcoatl to the earth,
to sort people by birthplace, like they are weeds
to sort people by colors, like they are beads
to sort people by heirloom, like they are seeds
A mariposa wonders why?

The gentle people sang and their songs passed easily through that wall
They played music, and either side could dance.
Speaking with smiles and songs
that transcended language and culture,
they told stories of separation and courage,
that inspired and touched each of the gentle people,
no matter where they stood on that divide.

Their singing and dancing and speaking made those ugly pillars dissolve.
They were just places between the spaces to cast welcome shade.
And there were faces of friends in the spaces.
Space enough for arms to reach through and touch.
To make a hug of two gentle people,
sandwiching an irrelevant pillar.

But I am Mariposa de la Gente Amable.
I fly by my own laws
I freely cross your cruel walls
however high.
I just flutter my wings and fly!

Some of the gentle people brought wings to wear,
Cardboard butterflies of orange and black
Symbolic of migration unhindered by walls.
They danced and fluttered their paper wings
and dreamed of a time when there would be nothing dividing them,
no walls, or laws, or fear,
no Border Patrol, no Migra, no detention centers.
They danced and sang and dreamed.

Some would notice the profusion of real butterflies
that suddenly appeared that day in the hot desert sun
at the wall that divides Nogales.

Jeeni Criscenzo Although she recently retired from Amikas, a non-profit she founded that works to house homeless women and children, she continues to advocate for homeless people and housing justice. She was one of the founders of Women Occupy San Diego and remains active in supporting many progressive causes, locally and nationally. In 2006 she was the Democratic candidate for the 49th Congressional District, running against Darrell Issa. In 2016 she was named Women's History Month Local Hero by the Women's Museum of California. She is an avid gardener, relentless feminist, performance poet, columnist in San Diego Free Press and a proud grandmother.

DANCING TREES

The sea breeze claps her hands in the placid night
A biting shower of rain falling on my head;
The pale eye of the moon showing me her light
The wind and the rain made love in the boisterous night.
Slender trees wave their hands from afar
The voice of the wind singing in their leaves;
This fragile world reborn under a silver star
The head of the half-moon arose from her rest.
On the shores of the sea birds danced on rattling shells
In the heart of my soul a tree is born within me,
The valley of my mind is hard to find
A tree in my soul is hard to break.
The moon is lost in a dark veil of clouds,
The world dies in sin, despair, and disdain.
Heaven is near my soul when I kneel to pray
I watch the broken world that's blown away.

Gideon Cecil

POETRY IS MY SUGAR

Poetry the sugar in my
tea I drink daily
as I go
to sleep at nights
to dream of my
muses hidden
in the invisible
roof of my soul.
My muses come
like a sudden
shower of rain
writing in the blank
pages of my immortal memory.

I drink a Shakespearean
sonnet;
A Dante's Tercet,
A Homeric Ode,
A Virgil's Epic
And a Milton's Blank verse;
As 'Poetry Sugar' into my tea
that sets my soul free
invoking my muses to
write in my fragile mind
so free.

Modern inventions
brings terror to
our souls; hatred of nations
bombing of the innocent
hacking into banks.
Spying us like an invisible
God in our homes.
Poetry is the sugar
in my tea
the balm of my soul
the mirror of your
eyes that shows you the
destiny of your life
in the garden of your
soul.

Gideon Sampson Cecil was born on the 9th of May 1968 in Rose Hall
Town, Corentyne Berbice, Guyana. He holds a Bachelor and Master
of Divinity from Life Christian University in Tampa, Florida and a
degree in journalism. He is a college lecturer and freelance journalist.
His poetry was published in POUi X by The University of the West
Indies, Cave Hill Campus, Barbados the Muse Literary Journal India,
The Harbinger Literary Journal USA, The Chachalaca Review
England, Forward Journal London, Thirty West Publishing House,
The Blue Nib Literary Magazine and Alien Buddha Press.

Gideon Cecil

EMERGENCY

Today is a day of emergence
blue jays emerge from red oak nests
sunbeams emerge from ominous clouds
bumblebees emerge from gillyflowers
stockbrokers emerge from razor scars   Emergency!

Emergence of turtles sunning on floating logs
emergence of lovers sipping wine in outdoor cafes
emergence of spotted dogs frolicking in parks
emergence of orphans riding on shooting stars   Emergency!

Earthworms emerge from composted soils
undercover cops emerge from dumpster bins in alleys
federal grand juries emerge from dark bankrolls
convicts emerge from solitary isolation holes   Emergency!

Emergence of angry seas crash and squall
emergence of trees tremble and fall
emergence of smoke billows in every direction
emergence of sidewalks roll and crack
emergence of great chasms and sink holes
emergence of we won't take this any more
emergence of organize educate resonate
emergence of solidarity together
emergence of toppling statues of patriarchs
emergence of islands from the waves
emergence of laughter at midnight
emergence of dismantle the deep state
emergence of bankers crying like babies
emergence of babies dreaming of paradise
emergence of another glorious day of emergence

Today is a day of emergence!   Emergency!

John Curl 183

NO FEAR

We walk these darkened streets
in this time of shadows
secret agendas overshadow
professional liars debate
false priests lay the bait
gristly reapers lay in wait
but the foxes are speaking
no fear in the now and here.

Stockholders' hateful prayers
quicksand TV news muddle
blinding chinese puzzles
hidden societies pollute the air
spies lurk everywhere
swat teams staging raids
lawns and flower beds betrayed
but the rivers are speaking
no fear in the now and here

Cancer festers every wound
mobsters of philosophy devouring
dandelions beaten and cowering
dangerous to speak your mind
dreading what is hidden behind
dark power masterminds
eighty thousand peaceful protesters
tortured by peace officers
trap doors jerk open pitfalls
endless arbitrary wars
justice attacked by smirking birds
ravenous demons mincing words
but the mountains are speaking
the forests are speaking
the foxes are speaking
the rivers are speaking
no fear in the now and here.

John Curl has published fiction *The Co-op Conspiracy*, memoir *Memories of Drop City*, radical history *Indigenous Peoples Day; For All The People*; thirteen volumes of poetry including *Revolutionary Alchemy* and *Yoga Sutras of Fidel Castro*. His translations of classical Mayan, Aztec, and Quechua poets are collected in Ancient American Poets. His play *The Trial of Columbus* has had two productions. He has been chair of PEN Oakland, and has represented the USA at the World Poetry Festival.

John Curl

STRAY

I've got corky on my mind,
A sea of brown raised fists,
By my side.

Trails turned to rivers
With tears from my kind.

Dirt-field hands
Sustaining our lives.

Deep thoughts escaping,
to expand other minds.

We're the ones that build,
That pick, that teach,
That learn,
That clean, that kick,
That protect,
And fight to survive.
Young seeds exist to learn
By our side.
I'm the roots, the seeds,
The plants, the trees

I don't live on my knees
I take pride when I lean
I take the time to make it
Recite power left from elders
I spend time with the waves
I observe how the play

Ocean's my reminder
to not stray.

Anaid Carreno

XIKANA

On the question of what does that mean?
When asked about my right wrist
Answering is teaching so teach when you get questioned
And always question
Hispanic or herpanic ?
How about no one's panic?
Hispanic: "from Spain
Any person from Mexico, Puerto Rico, Cuba, south or central America
and or other Spanish culture or origin,
regardless of race."
So the fact that my ancestors before me have given their blood
as sacrifice to me isn't included?
Where is my indigenous origin
From Anahuac, to Aztlan and back ?
Where the people, speak more than one language
And are never ashamed to be who they are?
Latino: inclusive of all
"A person of Latin-American or Spanish-speaking descent."
Like a big pile of colorless rocks
It doesn't explain where I've been and what I've done
This can't be where I come
Should I pick other
But then what do I mean by that?
I share what I learn and learn what I can
Xikana: a chosen identify
it could also be Mexican American
But the Mexican in me is still resentful
Chosen identity
Chosen to have that power
That's what I want
That's what I am
That's what you can call me

Anaid Carreno

That's me
Tattooed on my right wrist because
That's the wrist I showed
When I joined the protest to
Find inequality, injustice, and intolerance
Unacceptable.
When I saw the connection to indigenous ways I saw my reflection
I'm one of many,
Xikana.
A mindset a philosophy inclusive of all
Transcending all social constructions
And loving of all
starting with what I couldn't
See before.

Anaid Carreno was born in Oceanside CA and moved throughout Northern California. Her family is from Oaxaca Mexico where she lived during her childhood. She received my B.A. at Sonoma State University in Sociology with a minor in Chican@/ Latin@ studies. She has been published in an anthology titled *Coiled Serpents- Poets Arising from the Cultural Quakes and Shifts of Los Angeles*. She has performed for Parking Lot Poets hosted by Raizes Collective and El Comalito Collective which motivated her to keep sharing her poetry. She wrote her first poem at age 12 and has continued to write throughout her life. She has hosted workshops and uses poetry as a way to heal and express everyday life.

INVENTARIOS ALTOS

Aquí,
en la prosa de estos huesos,
lo que el *arcanjo* desoyó
lo escucharon el hombre y la mujer
con mutuo magisterio.

Y fuimos todos por el mismo rumbo,
llenos de antepasados,
pletóricos de días cada cual
sobre el ansia nómada
del tiempo.

Parvadas de nubes
volaban por el océano
de la altura.

Bajo la nube de
la desesperación
la multitud, amigos:
el dolor.

Y yo elegí no estar podrido,
no ser
la sola sombra;

pero a pesar de tanta agitación de alas
en mi alrededor los humanos
eran piedras que no pudieron
pensarmás.

Benjamín Valdivia (1960) es Miembro correspondiente de la Academia Mexicana de la Lengua y es profesor en la Universidad de Guanajuato. Su obra se encuentra en más de 50 libros publicados en los géneros de poesía, novela, cuento, teatro y ensayo, tanto académico como literario. También se han publicado múltiples traducciones que ha hecho desde el inglés, francés, portugués, italiano, alemán y latín para diversos medios mexicanos y extranjeros. Otras de sus prácticas artísticas son la música, la fotografía y el teatro. Más detalles en www.valdivia.mx

Benjamin Valdivia

HIGH INVENTORIES

Here,
inside the prose of these bones,
which the *arcángel* disregarded
the man and woman listened
with mutual mastery.

And we all went the same way,
we all plenty of ancestors,
each of us overflowing with days
through the nomadic yearning
of time.

Flocks of clouds
flew through the ocean
of the skies.

Beneath the cloud of
hopelessness
the crowd, my friends:
the pain.

And I chose not to be rotten,
not to be
the only shadow;

but in spite of so much winged agitation
around me, the humans
were stones that could think
no more.

Translated from Spanish by Bill Grinager & Benjamin Valdivia

Benjamín Valdivia (1960) is a corresponding member of the
Mexican Academy of Language. At present, he is teaching at the
University of Guanajuato. Author of more than 50 books of poetry,
novel, short story, drama, and essay (both academic and literary).
He has received several international and national prizes. He
translated diverse pieces from English, French, Portuguese, Italian,
German and Latin. Other artistic interests of his are music,
photography and theater. More information at: www.valdivia.mx

Benjamin Valdivia

189

NEO LUDDITES

I wish I could write
about the infinite blue
of the Atlantic
stretching away from Crane's
the crisp air
& low slant of the sun
a walk on the beach
is always fun
I'm with you
it's what we do
it cleanses our souls
it's the way we roll

but fuck it I can't go on
when there's so much wrong
Donald Trump
and his administration
a pack of liars
with alternative facts
that don't represent my nation
like Nazis before them
they come for the opposition
they come for the arts
they come for the poor
they have no heart

They deny climate change
even though it's fact
stick their heads in coal tar sands
It is now time to attack
I fight them each day
in whatever way I can
protest every injustice
don't let their lies stand
we march together
help out each other
resist every outrage
my sisters and brothers

Blaine Hebbel

THE PRESIDENT (NOT MINE) AT THE ECLIPSE

It's not because he is unaware
it's clearly because he just doesn't care
looks at the eclipse without the proper glasses
a pitiful example for the masses
smiles and smirks, thinks he's the sun god
when really he is nothing but a fraud
a mean spirited prick, a fake tan fool
doesn't care about what kids learn in school
setting a piss poor example
even for those who believe his lies
still can't wear correct length ties
distracting the public at every chance
deflecting scrutiny of his Russian dance
and now he rejects the dreamers
thinks of them as "bad hombre" schemers
this country was built with immigrant toil
but he even refuses to take care of our soil
he will see that climate change is real
but as hurricanes Harvey, Irma and Maria
deal violent blows to our nation
the president, (not mine)
is on another golf vacation

Blaine Hebbel Poet, activist and Ipswich native has been fighting social injustice since the 60s. He's read as a member of the Poets' Mimeo Cooperative in Burlington, VT and on the *Poemair* show on KUOR FM. He's a member of the Boston OccuPoets & has published four chapbooks, *Poems From the Shore, The Occupy Poems, Cracking Up* and *Poems of Resistance*. His work has appeared in publications, including Firehouse 15, Poesis, Oddball, Zig Zag Folios II, Bagel with the Bards #8 and Stone Soup Presents Fresh Broth. He started his publishing house, Ring of Bone Press, in 2011, with the mission to bring the "American Voice" to readers by publishing local, under discovered poets and writers. The first book, *Wild Women of Lynn,* was released in 2014 and the second, *Mad Men of Lynn* was published in 2017.

Blaine Hebbel

PANDEMONIUM

I'm making popcorn
POP!
propping the silk pillows on my couch
while Russia hacks the very fabric of our democracy
POP! POP!
I dim down the lights in my living room and
Puerto Rico's gone dark again
POP! POP!   POP!
Trump Tweets: *Little Rocket Man* MY BOMB'S BIGGER THAN YOURS
POP! POP! POP! POP! POP! POP! POP!
CNN Alerts: "*Pee Tape is an Out of Body Experience for Comey*"
POP! POP! POP!
Pop! Pop!
Pop!
P op
p...
Putin is coming to the White House
DING! goes the microwave
I empty the steamy kernels into a bowl
add a twist of Himalayan sea salt and a dollop of
I Can't Believe It's Not Butter
Kick off my shoes
shuffle across the plush rug
plop on the couch and watch
the new season of Scandal, starring Stormy Daniels

And before colluding with my favorite cabernet
I fill the glass all the way to the brim
and let it breathe

Anika Paris

CHILL

There's a bite in the air
in this desert coast terrain,
the weather as moody
as its people.
I wear scarves in June
carry a change of clothes
in case a fault line breaks its silence.
And while a sunny sky may provide
a backdrop for dreamers,
the elders of the earth, their
jagged bones in rocks and mountains,
point their noses toward heaven,
bend their backs against the sea,
reminding us Mother Nature
has a temper.

Anika Paris is a platinum songwriter and recording artist, HOLA award-winner for *Outstanding Music in a Musical*, and nominated for the *International Latin Poetry Award* for Woven Voices with *Scapegoat Press*. Her poems appeared in *KC Star, Helicon Nine Editions, Gival Press, Half Shell Press*, and *VAGABOND*. An author of two music education books with Hal Leonard, she is an adjunct professor teaching songwriting, lyric writing and performance at Musicians Institute, UCLA, and guest lectures at the Grammy, USC and more. A classically trained pianist, she composes for *Warner Bros. Television, Multi-stages*, and the *League of Professional Theatre Women.*

SHOCK TO THE SYSTEM

They

shocked

us

with

the

drop.

The whole world went cold and hot.
And in the midst of chaos
they dropped the real bomb.
And the constitution burst into flame
and Lady Liberty fell from her perch.
And the country convulsed
in a massive wave of hurt.
In this alt-right alternative reality,
in this KKK/Nazi punk fantasy;
where the good are pushed to extinction
and the bad serve with distinction.
What will it take from us
to defend our democracy?
What will it take from us
to end this fascist autocracy?
We've got to work like never before.
We've got to love like never before;

before

the

final

bomb

drops.

Susan "Spit-Fire" Lively

195

THE FORGOTTEN

She smiled sunnily at me,
mouth full of rotting teeth,
as if nothing were wrong,
this pretty black five year-old.

Lice danced in her hair,
amidst a sea of dandruff and debris.
Stains proclaimed themselves as
separate countries from her apparel.
And the smell of decay,
erupting like a dying rose,
from her skin and clothes.
Clinging delicately to her
strong bones,
eroding this fragile whole.

St. Louis screamed in the background
of this incongruously sunny day.
Light glinting off of Archways,
corporate skyscrapers,
and myriad tents of protest.
An occupation of the homeless,
or so they say.
But no one wants to play...

With the young girl bouncing from lap to lap,
fascination to fascination,
Seemingly unattached
to any parental figure.
Paint and dirt warring on her innocent face,
wisdom of a thousand hard days
peering from her gaze.
The pain of poverty
stamped like a brand of rejection
across her space.

Susan "Spit-Fire" Lively

Does she know she's in mortal danger?
This precious little homeless angel,
sleeping beneath the starry lights of greed.
Another lost soul in this lost city,
another victim wandering among the neglected,
hidden within the missing.
A shadow on the sidewalk,
a taint on the glory,
of this fading nation-flower,
where 1 in 6 live in poverty.
And 45 million live like this,
abandoned by the hour.
But she's just a kid,
she's just a kid.

What she must go through every day.
How will she eat, where will she sleep,
how will she survive?
Will she even come out of this alive?
What does the future hold for her?
What does the world have in store for her?
Lying on the concrete steps of Kiener Plaza –
a little girl dreams of a better future,
a little girl dreams that she is not lost,
a little girl dreams that she is not forgotten.

Susan "Spit-Fire" Lively is an award-winning poet; writer, spoken word artist, model, producer, visual artist, photographer, educator, and activist. Her poetry and short stories have appeared in *"Head to Hand"*, *"The Pen"*, *"The East St. Louis Monitor"*, *"Drumvoices Revue"*, *"SIUE News"*, *"Big Bridge"*, *"Static Movement"*, *"Postcard Shorts"*, *"No Vacancy"*, the *"She Chronicles"*, and *"Crossing the Divide"*. Lively produces the shows "First Bloom" and "Women For Peace", and "100 Thousand Poets & Musicians for Change – St. Louis". In 2016 she became an Officer of Urb Arts' Executive Board. In 2017 Susan produced the St. Louis leg of the international event "Poets & Musicians Against Trump" (with John Blair).

L'esecuzione
The Execution

L'occhio fisso lo scatto	The staring eye the wrathful
Iroso del ragno goloso	Sprint of the gluttonous spider
Spumeggia zampetta trascina	Foaming as it drags the weightless
Leggera la mosca impigliata	Leg of a captured fly
Dove la vuole prima	Where it wants to be before
Della mischia micidiale	The deadly scuffle
Ricamo d'ali sulle corde	Its embroidered wings up against the ropes
E poi più avvinta nel cuore	And then bound ever more tightly in the heart
Della ragnatela oltre la soglia	Of the web beyond the threshold
Dell'osillazione senza più segni	Of unruffled swing
Di scompiglio nel ruvido silenzio	In that coarse silence
Dell'esecuzione.	Of execution

Walter Valeri

Stranamente negli intervalli
Strangely Enough Commercial

Stranamente negli intervalli	Strangely enough commercial
pubblicitari annunciano il virtuoso	breaks announce a virtuous
medicamento scoperto	balm designed
per l'anoressica bambina a cui	for anorexic little girls
chi dà il seno piange volando in cielo	to whom nursing mothers cry as they rise to heaven
ed è un concerto d'ossa	a concert of bones
nel canale accanto con la signora	is broadcast next channel with a lady
che serenamente invita gli obesi	serenely calling on the obese
ad una vita se non di stenti	not to follow a life of hardship
serena fra le braccia della madre chiesa	but of serenity within the arms of mother church
poi si torna ai bombardamenti	then back to the bombings
(oh i bombardamenti!)	(oh, the bombings!)
le granate, le schegge telefoniche	grenades, telephone shrapnel
la raccolta di fondi paradossale	paradoxical fundraising telethons
un cimitero a cielo aperto su tutti e	an open sky cemetery over everyone and
su Bagdad.	over Baghdad.

Walter Valeri is a poet, playwright, director, dramaturge and translator whose works have been published, translated and performed on many occasions. From 1980 to 1996 he worked with Nobel laureate Dario Fo and his wife Franca Rame, serving as their personal assistant. In 1981 a collection of his poetry "*Canzone dell'amante infelice*" was awarded the prestigious "*Mondello*" International Literary Prize. He taught at Harvard University from 2000 to 2006, and his essay *Epic Theater, Comic Mode: Understanding Italian Society through the works of Dario Fo and Franca Rame* appeared in the *Set the stage!* (Yale University Press,  2008). Most recent theater and poetry books *May name/Il mio nome* (Qudu libri, 2015) *Parodie del Buio* (Società Editrice "Il Ponte Vecchio, 2017") and *Arlecchino e il profumo dei soldi/Harlequin and the scent of money* (Società Editrice "Il Ponte Vecchio", 2018. He currently teaches at Boston Conservatory at Berkelee, and directs the international Poetry, Video and Visual Arts Summer festival *L'orecchio di Dioniso* produced by the cities of Forlì and Cesenatico, Italy, since 2016.

Walter Valeri

199

Zero Visibility

time to watch
the roses, time to yank
a meditation

from the garden.
time to take a deep breath
and smell cold

morning air.
time for zero visibility
as a wrath of sea mist

crosses the roof,
defiling transmitters
and proving yet again

we're not prepared
to see what has become
of us. time to sweep

the deck of fallen leaves
and pick lemons
hidden in thick boughs.

zero tolerance
for refuge, zero
reason, the land

does not welcome
a stranger, not a man
or woman, not a child

or a wild/wise
dream, close your voice,
continue to watch

the rose, draw
blinds, bolt the door,
you came here

first, this is your
land, don' let
the poor and homeless

trample your serene
garden, pick a
rose petal, turn on

the hose
and stand firm,
give a good soaking

to your sins

Photo credit: Ben Sykes

Neeli Cherkovski was born in Los Angeles and attended Los Angeles State College (now Cal State Los Angeles). He is the author of many books of poetry, including *Animal* (1996), *Leaning Against Time* (2005), *From the Canyon Outward* (2009), and *The Crow and I* (2015). He is the co-editor of *Anthology of L.A. Poets* (with Charles Bukowski) and *Cross-Strokes*: Poetry between Los Angeles and San Francisco (with Bill Mohr). He has also published bilingual editions in Austria, Mexico, and Italy. A facsimile edition of one of his notebooks was published by Viviani Edizione in Verona, Italy. Cherkovski also wrote biographies of Lawrence Ferlinghetti and Charles Bukowski, as well as the critical memoir Whitman's Wild Children (1988). His papers are held at the Bancroft Library, University of California, Berkeley. Cherkovski received the 2017 Jack Mueller Poetry Prize awarded at the Jack Mueller Festival in Fruita, Colorado. He has lived in San Francisco since 1974.

BOAT PEOPLE

The friends we elected
In the secret ballot of the ancient heart
Went about their business then
In Dachau... Auschwitz and Belsen –
And so they purged us of our darkest dream
Of the Carpenter and The Cross.

Now comes the dawn of a godless day
There's no cross upon the door;
And each must choose his way
his weapons and his law.
With strychnine in the flour
and young blood upon the snow;
With spades for blades in the jungle heat
fine bones upon the floor.

Can you recall the slavers' barque –
the years of tears and blood beneath the deck;
in the true story of the modern dark
only the colours and the coasts have changed.
Protecting
          Innocence
                    Inner sins
                              Innocents

Patrick A. Harford

THE HOUSE OF LORDS

Sky's getting crowded
Above the House of Lords;
The markers of the hungry hearts
Racing between the capitals of the world
Are tracks on a limited sky

The day's oil slicks
On sea and sky – through the heavens and
Beyond the stars
Spell the end of Endeavour
Cook's legacy – dead seals,
Blood on the ice, the Tahitian spirits
Circling like birds of prey
Over the carcass of civilisation
lying dead below
teeming with the maggot millions
who have occupied the fatty corpses
that lie beside the lifeless rivers
and seas of a dying world.

And all the while
as the niches are emptied
the first amoeba in the virtual world
has already been hatched by forgetful man.
Complexity and cooling
Contradict then complement the warring factions.

Patrick A. Harford is an Australian and earth scientist. His work takes him throughout the globe – so Patrick experiences many places and many forms of labor. Patrick has kept his youthful commitment to poetry for over 50 years now – through poetry Patrick chronicles those places of our world, its beauties, truths, and its iniquities. Patrick's poems present places and people. Most have scars from centuries of war and conflict, and the lashings of huge wealth amid grinding poverty. Patrick's poems are his guides, his models, and they deal with his demons.

Patrick A. Harford

You Call It Prayer

Ashes
Night terrors
Images of a pale Jesus
Flashing through the sky

I lie awake and think the moon
has turned maroon
or maybe just plain red.
I imagine it now the color of dead.

I hear sounds that are thousands
of miles away, yet all familiar,
like a hand grenade rolling
across the floor, preparing
to spray shards of glass
into our collective throat.

Is there a difference
between war and peace
when you've never known
what dress peace will even wear
to the victory party?

I used to see towers falling
every time I closed my eyes.
Now they're gone and replaced
with a vision of dust covered bodies.

You kneel and pray
even as you cheer the fall
of bomb after bomb after bomb.
Do you even know
what time it is in Damascus?

Eric Allen Yankee

203

THIS IS HOW YOU MANUFACTURE A BULLET

A bullet is made with skin
   hanging off the sides.
First it's given a coat of blood
   and then someone kisses the tip,
and whispers, "Someday
   you'll make a fine kill."
A bullet is made by watching hours
   of little pieces roll down a line
and into the gun that sacrifices
   a woman's children
as they wait for her to return
   late each night.
A bullet is dipped in spit
   and given the name
of a future murderer
   who will shoot it out

and into someone's fate.
   The clock ticks down
and the whistle blows,
   time cards clink,
and someone goes home –
   and they load their gun,
and open their mouth,
   and manufacture a bullet,
because letting time pass
   and watching metal drop
just wasn't in the picture
   they imagined for their life.

Eric Allen Yankee is a member of the Revolutionary Poet's Brigade of Chicago. His work appears in *The People's Tribune, CC+D, Crab fat, Ygdrasil, The Miscreant, Sweet Wolverine, Writing Raw, The Fem,* and *Overthrowing Capitalism: Volume 2* and has recently been nominated for the prestigious Pushcart Poetry Award. He is also co–editor in chief of *Caravel Literary Arts Journal* (www.caraveljournal.org).

Eric Allen Yankee

THE GOOSE AND THE GANDER

MLK said: my country
Is the greatest
Purveyor of violence
In the world.
H. Rapp Brown said
Violence is
American as
Cherry pie.

Our foreign affairs
Perpetual war
Our domestic policy
War on poverty

Violent video games
Easy internet access
Violent movies
Easy gun access

We are taught
Might makes right
Kill the enemy
Imperialism for God and glory

Indian genocide
Broken treaties
Chattel slavery
No reparation no compensation

Invade Afghanistan
Take Iraq, bomb Libya & Syria
American exceptionalism
Record school shootings

Malcolm X said
The chickens
Have come
To roost

So, if we glorify
Violence abroad
Then we are justifying
Domestic violence

What's good for the goose
        Is good for the gander

Julio Rodriguez As the Conga Poet I have featured in many of Los Angeles Poetry venues. I played in San Francisco and Santa Rosa with Masaba Hood of the Last Poets. Opened up for music bands, featured live on KPFK radio. I produced two CDs, I am Free and Sonrisa Latina in 2014. My greatest thrill is being a street musician.

Julio Rodriguez ~ Conga Poet

206

THE OIL ROAD

I

Chorus: *The oil road*
let down road
the lifeless road

...And Scheherazade told me
looking into the future: "Don't open that box".

It contains the tales of war to control
the black gold   the air-water gold
the green gold   to control.

"Please, for now, do not open that box."
Let me nurture the child I see in your eyes.

Let it be the only reason to be a warrior
to stop the fire rain of your tears.

II

Chorus*:*   *The oil road*
the comfort road
the empty road

What does it matter this street
the far away boulevard in another country
or historic route 66.

We smear the oil of our gaze
giving streets a dead name.

Antonieta Villamil

We color the road oil-red
letting us peek from comfort windows.

The oil road knows our destination
the wide network of its labyrinth
connecting our steps   to a depleting place.

III

                                        Chorus: *The oil road*
                                                   the toxic road
                                           con dreamland road

What does it matter
your vehicle or my car!   Our furnished
caskets flying down lanes
and moonlit walk-sides
where children inhale gasoline

or how the terrain of a country
lets you drive   adrift from winter's heat
to a land pasted on to the silence
of smelting rocks under summer knife-rains.

It matters that we belong
to a tribe that migrates.   The tribe
that roams the earth   the universe
all the way to the core of change.

                                        Chorus: *The oil road*
                                                    a dirty load
                                            blind alley road

Sweat Lodge for Pachamama

Ancestors of air and water listen to our plea
Ancestors of earth and fire witness this wound

Chorus: Pachamama Pachamama
Tunka Shila tunka-hea chewo kielo
Pachamama Pachamama

We dig out our hearts looking
for the stone of ancestors hands in our chest

Find ourselves ageless and burning fast
in the long roads of their fingers

We enter the gatehouse and as we sweat
the Arctic melts in our veins

Naked from pride we roam under volcanic rocks
looking for the sign in the flames of earthy womb
touch ancient fever with the ice of our forehead

Ancestors inside the rocks let your light
in torrents of song   stir us into dislodge of capitalist usury

Blinks in the sky the constellation Phoenix
as these words heal our lament into outrage
inflame our fever with the strength of all voices

Tonight your crescent eyes drench the night
we daydream the dream of mother earth
witness the injury   grassroot to heal her wounds

Ancestors inside the rocks unite our hands
Ancestors inside the stones heal this wound

Antonieta Villamil is an AWA International Award Winning bilingual poet with over 11 published books. She focuses her writing on the forgotten ones and honors them with a persistence that compels us to hear their voices. The Cervantes Institute of New York and Literacy Now awarded the "14 International Latino Book Award 2012" for her book "Soluna en Bosque: Conjuros Para Invocar El Amor", the "International Poetry Award Gastón Baquero 2001" in Spain with "Acantilados Del Sueño".

Antonieta Villamil

TRUMP'S TROJAN HORSE

Homer didn't live long enough

To tell of Trump's White House

Which is his Trojan horse

From which all the President's men

Burst out to destroy democracy

And install corporations

As absolute rulers of the world

Ever more powerful than nations

And it's happening as we sleep

Bow down, oh Common Man

Bow down!

Lawrence Ferlinghetti is a prominent voice of the wide-open poetry movement that began in the 1950s, Lawrence Ferlinghetti has written poetry, translation, fiction, theater, art criticism, film narration, and essays. Often concerned with politics and social issues, Ferlinghetti's poetry countered the literary elite's definition of art and the artist's role in the world. Though imbued with the commonplace, his poetry cannot be simply described as polemic or personal protest, for it stands on his craftsmanship, thematics, and grounding in tradition. Ferlinghetti's *A Coney Island of the Mind* continues to be the most popular poetry book in the U.S. It has been translated into nine languages, and there are nearly 1,000,000 copies in print. A 50th anniversary edition was published by New Directions in 2008. The author of poetry, plays, fiction, art criticism, and essays, he has a dozen books currently in print in the U.S., and his work has been translated in many countries and in many languages. His most recent poetry books are *Americus Book I* (2004), *Poetry As Insurgent Art* (2007), and *Time of Useful Consciousness* (2012) all published by New Directions. His most recent work of poetry is the chapbook *Blasts Cries Laughter* (2014).

✣ *This poem was first published in the Nation Magazine in 2017.*

Lawrence Ferlinghetti

ESSERE ACQUA

Nella lotta contro la tirannia e l'oppressione
Dobbiamo essere liquidi, senza forma, come l'acqua.

Senza acqua non ci può essere vita,
Quindi sì – Mni Wiconi – L'acqua è vita

... e dobbiamo essere come l'acqua
Ciascuno di noi
Una preziosa goccia.

Sola, fragile, forse la dimensione di una lacrima
In grado di essere cancellata con il movimento di un bastone
Ma insieme, con il potere degli oceani al nostro comando
Possiamo essere la marea che solleva tutte le imbarcazioni dalla loro iniquità.

Ancora, possiamo raggiungere questo solo attraverso l'amore.

Per quale motivo è, la vita, senza amore,
La corrente battente della nostra umanità?

Non siamo stati forse generati per nessun altro scopo
Che amarci l'un l'altro?

L'amore è l'intero senso della vita
Perché senza amore la vita non ha senso.

Sappiamo tutti che questo è vero.

Più amiamo,
Più in armonia siamo con la vita

... e questo significa essere attivi con amore in questo mondo.

L'acqua che scorre non è stantia,
piscina stagnante, murata

Mark Lipman

Be Water

In the struggle against tyranny and oppression
we must be formless, shapeless – like water.

Without water there can be no life,
So yes – Mni Wiconi – Water is Life

... and we must be like water
each and every one of us
a precious drop.

Alone, fragile, perhaps the size of a teardrop
able to be wiped off with the flick of a baton
yet together, with the power of oceans at our command
we can be the tide that lifts all boats from their inequity.

Yet, we can only achieve this through love.

For what is life without love,
        the beating current of our humanity?

Were we not put here for any other purpose
        than to love one another?

Love is the whole meaning of life
        for without love life is meaningless.

We all know this to be true.

The more we love,
        the more in harmony we are with life

... and that means to be active with love in this world.

Flowing water never goes stale,
yet a stagnant pool, walled off

Mark Lipman

213

crivellata da gasdotti,
ammorbante.

Quello che fa la differenza è l'amore.

Così come l'acqua, noi diffonderemo e copriremo questa terra
portandoovunque ci sia bisogno, l'amore.

Se è necessario negli aeroporti,
Inonderemo i terminal con i nostri corpi.

Se è necessario al municipio,
I tubi esploderanno dalla pressione del nostro vapore.

E se è necessario per le strade,
Pioveremo su centinaia di città
bonificando questo regime con il tuono
Della nostra ingovernabilità.

Come tsunami verremo,
dal North al South Dakota
E dovunque ce ne sia bisogno.

Perché è quello che fai
Quando sei veramente motivato dall'amore.

Quindi, siamo amore - siamo vita - siamo acqua, miei amici.

✢ *Ispirato da un'intervista a Bruce Lee intitolata "Be Water, My Friend".*

Translated by Maria Elena Daneli

and riddled with pipelines
can only fester with disease.

What makes the difference is love.

So like water, we will spread and cover this land
   putting ourselves wherever love is needed.

If it's needed in the airports,
   we'll flood the terminals with our bodies.

If it's needed at city hall,
   the pipes will burst from the pressure of our steam.

And if it's needed in the streets,
   we will rain down on hundreds of cities
   drenching this regime with the thunder
                 of our ungovernableness.

As a tsunami we will come,
   to the Dakotas
   and anywhere else we need to be.

For that is what you do
   when you are truly motivated by love.

So be love – be life – be water, my friends.

* Inspired by an interview with Bruce Lee entitled, "Be Water, My Friend."

216

HUMBLENESS

They say the greatest gift of all,
comes from your humbleness.

And they say the greatest joy of all,
can never be expressed.

And they say two wrongs don't make a right,
but that's self-evident.

And they say true love will conquer all
and I only pray they're right.

And if you see a mighty tree
out in the forest,

never dare you cut it down.
Oh, can't you tell the world's in distress?

No matter how much you ever earn,
you'll still die a lonely old mess.

So if you wanna get it right,
try trading in tenderness.

And they say the greatest love of all,
comes with sincerity.

And they say the greatest peace for all,
lies in equality.

And they say the good will always win,
but that depends on who writes the history.

And I've got a sad feeling, my friend,
That it'll never be you and it'll never be me.

And they say the greatest gift of all,
comes from your humbleness.

And they say the greatest joy of all,
can never be expressed.

And they say two wrongs don't make a right,
but that's self-evident.

And they say true love will conquer all
and I only pray they're right.

And they say true love will conquer all
and I only pray they're right.

(Chords: G Am C Em / Fmaj Am C A7)

Mark Lipman, founder of the press VAGABOND; recipient of the 2015 Joe Hill Labor Poetry Award; winner of the 2016 International Latino Book Awards for *The Border Crossed Us (an anthology to end apartheid)*; a writer, poet, multi-media artist and activist, is the author of seven books, most recently, *Imposing Democracy; Poetry for the Masses;* and *Global Economic Amnesty.* Co-founder of the Berkeley Stop the War Coalition (USA), Agir Contre la Guerre (France) and Occupy Los Angeles, he has been an outspoken critic of war and occupation since 2001. Mark uses poetry to connect communities to the greater social issues that affect all of our lives, while building consciousness through the spoken word.

Mark Lipman

217

"NEVER FORGET THAT EVERYTHING HITLER DID IN GERMANY WAS LEGAL."
Martin Luther King, Jr.
Letter from a Birmingham Jail, 1963

INDEX OF ARTWORK

VAGABOND

"EXTREME – a global Canto General "of all the peoples struggling for freedom."
.... Open it anywhere. The anthology is possessed with a kind of bibliomancy –
handbook, roadmap, guerrilla manual, prophetic guide – the weight and volume
of truth-to-power combusts into consciousness."

~ Richard Cambridge

"As political psychotics play with biocide to maintain a failed economic system
together with 19th century nationalism, we can be grateful for the poetry of
truth tellers... and this bouquet of truth telling..."

~ Blasé Bonpane, Ph.D.

"Prophetic poets are the courageous and compassionate vanguard of a better
world to come even in our bleak time. This book keeps our flame lit and our
fire burning!"

~ Dr. Cornel West